COXON BELLEEK

Wooster's Elegant China

David Broehl

To Ron —
I was a pleasure to have
the opportunity to work with and get to
know you. Best wishes!
Dave

The Wooster Book Company
where minds and imaginations meet

WOOSTER, OHIO
2009

*Frontispiece and back cover: The only known porcelain china plaque of the Coxon Belleek logo.
Courtesy of the Wayne County Historical Society.*

COXON BELLEEK
Wooster's Elegant China

www.coxonbelleek.com

© 2009 David Broehl

The Wooster Book Company
205 West Liberty Street
Wooster, Ohio 44691
330.262.1688
www.woosterbook.com

Book designed by Jeff Hentosz and David Wiesenberg
Printed in the United States of America by Wooster Printing & Litho, Wooster, Ohio

Mixed Sources
Product group from well-managed
forests, controlled sources and
recycled wood or fibre
www.fsc.org   Cert no. SW-COC-003085
© 1996 Forest Stewardship Council

FSC

ISBN: 978-1-59098-193-1

ACKNOWLEDGEMENTS

Many people helped in the production of this book and their contribution is greatly appreciated:

Ward and Dorothy Konkle who were the first true historians of the Coxon Belleek Company. The Konkles wrote, lectured and collected samples of Coxon Belleek china on behalf of the Wayne County Historical Society in the 1970s and the 1980s.

The Wayne County Historical Society sponsored two special exhibits in the 1980s and again in the 1990s. China was loaned to the society for each exhibit, and pictures were taken of each piece of china. Many of these pictures appear in this book courtesy of the Society. Thanks to the Konkles who organized the first event and also to Ethel Parker and Lee Meyer who organized the second exhibit with the author.

All the individuals and families who loaned china to the two exhibits sponsored by the Wayne County Historical Society and gave permission for their china to be photographed. In addition, all the individuals and families who permitted the author to photograph china from their personal collections.

George A. Limbocker Jr., grandson and Rebecca Coxon Dyson, granddaughter of J. Frederick and Vivian Coxon for their kindness in sharing family pictures and memories.

Ric "Chico" Martinez was responsible for the majority of the photographs of the individual pieces of china. Ric felt that the pictures should be taken outside in the natural light. Capturing the appropriate light was crucial to the clarity of the photographs.

Sally Barnes, Joan and John Bupp and Jim Norton for their expertise in developing the Coxon Belleek price guide of 2008 for this book.

Hope Reynolds, Margo Broehl and Shelly Hancock for their expertise and time in the process of editing this book. The book reads so much better with their help and guidance.

Emily Rufener who typed the first draft of this book from dictation and saved the author countless hours of time.

David Wiesenberg of The Wooster Book Company and Heather Kuntz Henthorne of Wooster Printing & Litho who both provided critical layout and printing expertise in the production of this book.

Finally, there were several books that were crucial for the author's understanding of the china and pottery industry. Mary Frank Gaston in her book *American Belleek* shared details about the American Belleek companies and the china industry with such a high level of knowledge and expertise. The book *China and Glass in America 1880–1980* by Charles Venable, Ellen Denker, Katherine Grier, Stephen Harrison and Tom Jenkins (photographer) gave a comprehensive historical perspective of the china and pottery industry that was invaluable. Regina Lee Blaszcyk in her book, *Imagining Consumers: Design and Innovation from Wedgewood to Corning* illuminated the business side of the china and pottery industry. And special thanks to Ellen Paul Denker for her book, *Lenox China: Celebrating a Century of Quality: 1889 through 1989*. In addition, the newspapers from Trenton, New Jersey; Kokomo, Indiana; and Wooster, Ohio proved to be invaluable sources of information about the Coxon family.

CONTENTS

The Tragic Story of Nellie Coxon ❧ Manufacture of Pottery and Pottery Tariff ❧ Coxon Family Obituaries ❧ Coxon Family Geneaology ❧ Coxon Family Tree ❧ Additional Articles ❧ Walter Lenox

PREFACE

The story of the Coxon Belleek Company has intrigued Wooster residents, china collectors and amateur historians for many years. The beauty and quality of Coxon Belleek china is unparalleled. Individual pieces and sets of Coxon Belleek are highly prized and sought by collectors. The wide array of patterns, the use of gold and hand painting in the design, and the translucence of the china itself are unique to Coxon Belleek.

But, within six short years of operation, the company disappeared off the face of the earth with no evidence of its existence except for the samples and sets of the china itself!

There were a myriad of challenges in writing a book about the Coxon Belleek Company. The company was only in existence from 1925–1931, and because of Coxon Belleek's precipitous reverse in fortune with all three owners leaving Wooster soon after the demise of the company, there were no records, brochures, pamphlets, business files, pictures, equipment or china saved from the company itself. With the advent of the Depression and WWII, the focus of people's lives switched from the community

to the self. All people in the 1930s and 1940s were worried about survival, not the history of a fledgling business in a small town.

The Wayne County (Ohio) Historical Society, through loyal members Ward and Dorothy Konkle, had begun research on the company and gathered a small collection of Coxon Belleek china for display in the 1970s and 1980s. However, many questions and issues about the Coxon Belleek Company remained unanswered. These included:

Who were the owners of the company: J. Fred, Edward T. and Edward B. Coxon? Where did they live and work before coming to Wooster, Ohio? And why did they choose Wooster to establish their company?

What impact did the business partnership between their father, Jonathan Coxon Sr., and Walter Lenox (of Lenox China) have on the establishment and operation of Coxon Belleek? Who was Walter Lenox and who was Jonathan Coxon Sr.?

What was Belleek china? How difficult was it to make and how did Coxon Belleek learn to make it, so quickly and so well? Did other companies make it?

What was the history of the pottery and china industry as it relates to the operation of Coxon Belleek?

How did Coxon Belleek start, how did it operate, how did it sell and distribute its wares, and how and why did it fail?

Coxon Belleek had only two named patterns out of hundreds of patterns. The remainder of the patterns was identified by a complicated numbering and lettering system. What was the methodology for this numbering system?

What happened to the three owners, J. Fred, Edward T. and Edward B. and their families after the demise of the company?

All of these questions will be addressed, and answered to the extent possible, in this book. The book is meant to interest china and Coxon Belleek collectors, business and family historians, and the citizens of Wooster and Wayne County, Ohio. It portrays a microcosm of life beginning with the optimism of the Roaring 20s and moving into the pessimism and anxiety of the Depression Era. Coxon Belleek is an American story.

It was a pleasure to research and write, and hopefully it will be a pleasure to read.

INTRODUCTION

Coxon Belleek is a story of great expectations and family pride but, ultimately, a story of tumbling fortunes and family tragedy. It is a microcosm of the optimism of the "Roaring 20s" turning into the pessimism of the Depression of the 1930s.

Although incorporated on December 11, 1925, the Coxon Belleek China Company was not just the start of a new business in Wooster, Ohio. It was the continuation of a family dynasty in the art of china making. The story actually begins in the mid 1800s with a young Jonathan Coxon emigrating from England to New Jersey and starting as an apprentice with various china companies at the outset of the development of the china industry in the United States. After enhancing his knowledge of the principles of making china over twenty years with various companies, Jonathan partnered with Walter Lenox and established The Ceramic Art Company in 1889 in Trenton, New Jersey, which later became The Lenox China Company. Of the hundreds of fine china companies established in the United States since the mid 1800s, Lenox China is the most successful and longest lasting manufacturer of high quality china and remains in operation today.

Making china was in the blood and soul of the Coxon family. Although Jonathan sold out his share of The Ceramic Art Company in 1896 to Walter Lenox and went into semi-retirement in Trenton, every male member of Jonathan's progeny went on to produce fine and vitrified china for companies in New Jersey, Indiana, and Ohio from the late 1800s through the first half of the twentieth century. In fact, in the late 1800s and early 1900s, William G., Edward T., Jonathan Frederick, Theodore and George Coxon went to Kokomo, Indiana and worked in a vitrified china company, Great Western Pottery, which became one of the largest employers of Kokomo and the largest porcelain company in Indiana. William, Edward and J. Fred each became successful businessmen and community leaders in Kokomo.

Two of the brothers, J. Fred and Edward T., along with Edward's son Edward B., started Coxon

3

Belleek in 1925. Why did the two brothers and the son leave a highly successful business based in Indiana to start a fledgling company in Wooster, Ohio? Although nothing is written to confirm the reasons, we can speculate. One major reason was the optimism of the times. In the 1920s, there was an attitude in the United States that, with sufficient knowledge and hard work, a person could start a business, make it successful and become financially comfortable, if not wealthy. The American Dream was within the grasp of everyone. People were constantly starting new companies based upon the optimism of the times, and the Coxon sons were no different.

Another reason may have had to do with family pride. Jonathan Coxon Sr. was an American success story. He went from rags to riches, managed many china companies, and was a leader and beloved citizen in Trenton. However, the most successful venture in his career was the relatively brief seven-year partnership with Walter Lenox when they established The Ceramic Art Company in 1889. Lenox China, which evolved from Ceramic Art Company, grew to be a success primarily through the hard work, design skills and business foresight of Walter Lenox. However, Jonathan's contribution at the beginning of the venture was very important. He helped capitalize the company, organized and managed the plant, and also, most likely, devised and modified, with Walter Lenox, the formula for translucent Belleek china. Although we cannot attribute the development in the United States of this elusive formula to Jonathan Coxon alone, he was at the nexus of the development of this process, both with The Ceramic Art Company (Lenox) and with Ott and Brewer, another Trenton company famous for their Belleek ware.

In 1925, Coxon Belleek was incorporated in Wooster. By then, Lenox China was a world leader in the manufacture of fine china. There had to have been a feeling of "opportunity lost" on the part of the Coxon family. If Jonathan had remained with The Ceramic Art Company, would the successor company have been named "Lenox & Coxon China," "Coxon & Lenox China," or "Coxon China," not Lenox China? The competitive juices of the Coxon family may

have been a significant contributor to the desire to start a new fine china company in the mid 1920s using the Belleek formula.

Coxon Belleek was started in 1925 by J. Fred Coxon, his brother, Edward Coxon (both sons of Jonathan Sr.), and Edward's son, Edward Coxon Jr. The corporation was dissolved in September of 1932 although the factory actually closed in November of 1931. In these short six years, Coxon Belleek purchased land and a building, bought and installed equipment, hired between 50–75 employees, and developed a large list of over one hundred distributors nationwide. And, most significantly, it manufactured one of the finest examples of Belleek china that America has ever produced.

This book will explore how the company started, the operations of the company, the elements of manufacturing fine china, and the company's tragic ending. We will learn about the Coxon family, truly one of the leading families in the history of the manufacture of fine china. We will also explore the lives of Walter Lenox and Nellie Coxon, daughter of William Coxon, the oldest of the twelve Coxon children. We will explore life in the "Roaring 20s" and life during the Great Depression. And we will share with the reader many photographs of the glittering array of patterns of Coxon Belleek, Wooster's Elegant China.

SOURCES

∥ Ward and Dorothy Konkle, Co-Chairs, Wayne County Historical Society Exhibit, 1986 and various articles and presentations by the Konkles.

∥ David Broehl, Ethel Parker and Lee Meyer, Co-Chairs, Wayne County Historical Society Exhibit, 1997.

JONATHAN COXON SR.,
THE PATRIARCH AND HIS FAMILY

It would be impossible to write the history of the Coxon Belleek Company without exploring Jonathan Coxon Sr.'s life and that of his children. The name of Coxon was well known in ceramic and pottery circles in this country for more than a century. Charles Coxon, a relative of Jonathan, modeled hound-handled pictures and figures of dogs for Bennett & Brothers of Baltimore, Maryland in the 1850s.

Jonathan Coxon Sr., was an extraordinary leader and businessman. Arriving in the United States from England in 1844, he worked in the pottery and china industry for his whole life, over sixty years. He also led and encouraged all six of his sons to enter into the pottery and china industry, and they subsequently worked in New Jersey, Indiana and Ohio. These children include William G., Jonathan Frederick, Edward T., George H., Frank H., and Theodore. Edward T. and J. Fred, along with Edward's son, Edward Jr., were the founding partners of Coxon Belleek.

Jonathan Coxon was born in Longton, Staffordshire, England, and immigrated to the United States at age seven in May, 1844. He lived in Jersey City,

New Jersey, until 1857, when he went to South Amboy, New Jersey to work in a pottery. It was in South Amboy that he met his future wife, Miss Hannah Joshua, who was from Nantiglow, Wales. When Coxon was twenty-two, he and Miss Joshua were married at the Methodist Church in South Amboy. In 1860, the Coxons went back to Jersey City and remained there until 1863, at which time Jonathan enlisted in the Twenty-First New Jersey Volunteers, Company A.

Following the Civil War in 1865, the Coxons went to Trenton, where Jonathan was named a foreman at the Coxon and Thompson Company. The Coxon co-owner was Jonathan's Uncle Charles. David Goldberg in his monograph of Pioneer Potters and Potteries of Trenton, New Jersey says, "Charles Coxon was one of the best known and established potters in the United States when he arrived in Trenton in 1861. Charles also came from the Staffordshire area of England and worked in Jersey City and Baltimore before he came to Trenton. In Baltimore, he was employed as senior modeler and is credited with creating a number of important works for Bennett's Pottery. One of his earliest employees was Jonathan."

Jonathan left Coxon and Thompson in 1868 to seek employment with The Mercer Pottery Company in Trenton, which was founded that year. Control of the Mercer Pottery Company was vested in John Thompson who was previously associated with Charles Coxon.

After leaving Mercer, he was next employed at Greenwood Pottery Company in Trenton, again as a foreman. Coxon learned yet another skill set because Greenwood was well known for pioneering the development of hotel china as well as for its artistic efforts in the development of high-quality china similar to Royal Worchester.

Subsequently in 1879, he was employed for a short period of time as a foreman by International Pottery in Trenton, which made white granite and related products.

After leaving International, he was employed at Ott & Brewer in Trenton where he eventually became superintendent after the previous superintendent, William Bromley Sr., left to go to Willets. William Bromley Jr. had come to Trenton from the Irish

Belleek factory in order to formulate the Belleek process for Ott & Brewer, and then enticed his father to leave Ireland and come to work at Ott & Brewer to finalize their version of Belleek china. It was at Ott & Brewer that Coxon met Walter Lenox for the first time while learning the technique of making Irish Belleek from William Bromley Sr.

In 1888, Coxon was the co-founder of Equitable Pottery Company in Trenton that manufactured sanitary wares. Equitable was eventually merged into The Trenton Potteries Company in which W.S. Hancock had an interest.

Then Jonathan Coxon partnered with Walter S. Lenox and started the Ceramic Art Company. Because of his previous relationship with Mr. Hancock at Equitable Pottery, it was Coxon who obtained the $4,000 loan from Mr. Hancock with which Ceramic Art Company was started. His partnership with Walter S. Lenox in the Ceramic Art Company (the precursor of Lenox China) began in 1889 and ended in 1896. The parting was amicable and was likely attributed to Coxon nearing the end of his career and Lenox still in the middle of his career.

Interestingly enough, Coxon sons William, Edward, George and Fred grew up in the pottery and one of their main tasks was to run to the bank for the gold coin that was used for decoration.

After leaving Ceramic Art Company, he became the Superintendent of Anchor Pottery and later Superintendent of Crescent Pottery, both in Trenton, where he remained until his final retirement. W.S. Hancock was one of the founders of Crescent, which gives more weight to the notion that it was Coxon who arranged The Ceramic Art Company loan.

Coxon was always active in community affairs. He served on the Trenton Common Council for three years, having been elected as a Republican from the First Ward. Later, he spent four years on the Mercer County Board of Chosen Freeholders, was twice Director of that group, and given a diamond pin upon his retirement. He spent thirteen years on the Park Board and was President for two terms. In addition, he was past minister of Loyal Lodge 131 of F.A.&M., past regent of Capital City Council, past commander of Aaron Wilkes Post No. 23 GAR, and member of Crescent Temple Mystic Shrine.

In the Trenton Evening Times, Friday, August 31, 1917, edition, an article appeared sharing the celebration of his 80th birthday. It indicates clearly the respect that Trentonians felt for him. "Jonathan Coxon, 80 years old, veteran potter, former councilman and freeholder, greeted by friends today. Mr. Coxon, who is numbered among Trenton's most famous citizens, is today celebrating the eightieth anniversary of his birth at his home. Members of the Coxon family and friends of Mr. Coxon are calling and offering congratulations, while postcard felicitations are many."

Jonathan's obituary states, "Jonathan Coxon died on September 4, 1919 at the age of 82. Funeral services for Jonathan Coxon were held from the home of his son-in-law, Hugh H. Trout, yesterday afternoon. Floral tributes were received from children, William G. Coxon and family; George Coxon and family; The Wooster Manufacturing Company, Fredericksburg, Ohio [owned by his son J. Fred]; and Walter A. Lenox."

It is informative that Walter Lenox showed his respect and concern by sending flowers. The relationship between Jonathan Coxon and Walter Lenox obviously remained strong and showed the deep respect held for each other. Mr. Lenox himself died shortly later in 1920 at the age of sixty-one.

The Coxons lived in Trenton, New Jersey, for many years and had twelve children. Eight children survived into adulthood. In addition, George Evans, later of Rittenhouse & Evans China, was a nephew of Jonathan Coxon and lived at the Coxon home for some time.

The eight children who survived into adulthood were:

1) William G., born July 23, 1860. He married Adele L. Dolle and they had five children: Nellie, Jonathan B., Hannah, Charlotte, and Adele. He died on August 3, 1937 in Kokomo, Indiana. He co-founded and was Superintendent at the Great Western Pottery Company in Kokomo for over thirty years. From this venture, he made a sizable fortune and retired.

2) Theodore B., born March 2, 1862 and died March 9, 1902 in Tiffin, Ohio, at the age of thirty-nine. He married Luella Smith, and it is not known if he had any children. He worked at Great Western Pottery Company in Kokomo with his brother William and then at Great Western's branch in Tiffin.

3) Frank H., was born on November 15, 1864 and died on Saturday, March 2, 1912 in Trenton at the age of forty-seven after a lingering illness. He was unmarried. He worked at Prospect Hill Pottery in Trenton.

4) Harriet A., born August 11, 1868. She married Joseph B. Erskine of Pittsburgh and Aspinwall, Pennsylvania. They had three children: Harold, Margaret and Florence. Mr. and Mrs. Erskine were not involved in the pottery and china business.

5) Edward T., born July 19, 1870 and died September 26, 1941 in Trenton, New Jersey. Edward married Mary B. and had a son, Edward B. Edward T. was a foreman of the Great Western Pottery Company. From this venture, he made a sizable fortune.

6) Anne K. was born on March 25, 1872 and married Hugh D. Trout. They had four children, Henry, Robert, Richard and Edward, and remained in the Trenton area. Mr. and Mrs. Trout were not involved in the china and pottery business.

7) George H. was born on March 25, 1874 and married Rebecca. They had two children, Ruth and Audrey. He stayed on at Ceramic Art Company and then Lenox China after his father left and then went on to become Superintendent of an electrical porcelain plant in Peru, Indiana.

8) John Frederick, born on June 28, 1879 and died on September 28, 1951. He married Vivian E., and they had three children, Lygustia, Vivian C. and Frederick K. He started his career at Great Western Pottery Company in Kokomo and then was named Superintendent of the Great Western's branch in Tiffin, Ohio, at the age of twenty-one. He also operated a small pottery in Fredericksburg, Ohio while living in Wooster, Ohio. He was the President of the Coxon Belleek Company. He was the youngest of the Coxon

children to survive to adulthood.

Jonathan and Hannah's other four children were Sarah, born on January 13, 1862, and died on July 2, 1862, less than one year old; John M., born on October 27, 1866, and died on April 3, 1878, at eleven years of age; Matthew born on September 12, 1876, and died on February 18, 1878, at one and a half years of age; and Albert, born on December 26, 1880, and died on August 24, 1889, at eight and a half years of age.

As is readily evident, the involvement of the Coxon family in Great Western Pottery Company of Kokomo was as significant as was Jonathan Coxon Sr.'s involvement in The Ceramic Art Company of Trenton. Four of the brothers worked in various capacities of the Kokomo company (William, Edward T., Theodore, and John Frederick), as well as Edward B., the son of Edward T.

Great Western Pottery Company was a large and successful enterprise. In the 1909, Howard History of Kokomo, Indiana, it says, "The Great Western Pottery Company was established in 1893 by its present owners, two Conradt brothers and [William G.] Coxon, who is the Superintendent. The original size was four kilns. It now operates ten kilns. The buildings cover 90,000 square feet. When the factory was first built, it was the only one west of Pittsburgh, Pa.. Nine years ago, this company secured the same kind of factory at Tiffin, Ohio, which has seven kilns and has practically the same output. The Kokomo plant employs 150 people, ninety percent of whom are skilled workmen. The payroll is about $10,000.00 per month. Their output is sanitary pottery ware and their shipments are in carload lots."

After gaining the experience and financial independence from working in the Great Western Pottery Company, coupled with obtaining the Belleek formula from their father and The Ceramic Art Company, J. Fred, Edward T. and Edward B. were ready to take on the new challenge of forming the Coxon Belleek Company.

SOURCES:

/// *The People Magazine*

/// Howard History of Kokomo, Indiana

/// *Kokomo Tribune*

/// *Preliminary Notes on the Pioneer Potters and Potteries of Trenton New Jersey, The First Thirty Years 1852–1882 (And Beyond)*, David J. Goldberg c. 1983 Trenton, New Jersey.

/// Ward and Dorothy Konkle

Belleek China

What is Belleek china? First manufactured in 1863, Belleek gets its name from the small town of Belleek, Ireland. What really made it possible to manufacture china in Ireland is that the Belleek area is rich in deposits of kaolin, a fine white clay, and also feldspar and flint. The more the early workers experimented with Belleek clay, the more astounded they became at its remarkable properties. They could do things previously thought impossible. They could create china with a soft, almost creamy, mother-of-pearl affect. To their amazement, the pieces retained a tough resilience that could withstand continuous daily use. In addition to this rich resource of fine white clay, the natives of the Belleek area were superb craftsmen and still are today. The exact formula of materials used to make Irish Belleek remains a secret, although U.S. china makers devised a similar formula for the American Belleek.

The porcelain body was invented by William H. Goss of Stoke on Trent, England, probably during the late 1850s. Porcelain manufacturing and the Belleek process was perfected by 1872 by McBirney & Company of Ireland who created the delicate, translucent ware by combining an exceptional porcelain with newly developed French glaze. The porcelain was parian ware characterized by its warm, creamy white surface. The iridescent glaze resembles mother-of-pearl.

Belleek porcelain was an instant success. In 1919, the Irish Times said of Belleek china: Its grace of design and delicacy of texture are an advertisement throughout the world of the skill and taste of Irish craftsmanship. With only a few interruptions through the years, that pottery has remained in operation from its founding until the present. Since 1920, the pottery has been named Belleek Pottery, Ltd.

Mary Frank Gaston, in her book *American Belleek*, says,

> Belleek became the name used to identify Irish porcelain, but that was not the intention of the factory. Belleek was used only to refer to the location of the pottery, and not to a particular form of porcelain. Today, although Belleek is technically defined by Webster's Dictionary as a type of pottery resembling porcelain, Belleek is more accurately considered a special type of porcelain.
>
> Irish Belleek was first exhibited in the United States at the Philadelphia Exposition in 1876. One Trenton, New Jersey pottery company, Ott & Brewer, displayed an ivory porcelain decorated to look like the Irish Belleek at the same exposition. Ott & Brewer must have admired the

Irish porcelain and decided to try to imitate it. Although Ott & Brewer was successful in making parian, an ivory porcelain, the owners were not completely satisfied with their attempts at duplicating Irish Belleek. This is evident because in 1882, six years after the exposition, they hired William Bromley Jr. from the Irish Pottery itself, to teach them the technique. William's father, William Bromley Sr. had been instrumental in developing the Irish porcelain. William Sr. came to Trenton in the next year, 1883, with some other potters from the Irish factory because his son was not able to implement the technique himself. With the senior Bromley's expertise, Ott & Brewer was able to produce a porcelain with the same characteristics as the Irish Belleek; a thin translucent body, light in weight, with a pearly iridescent glaze.

Barber, in 1893, states that "Ott & Brewer porcelain was fully equal to the Irish Belleek, and that in color and lightness of weight, the products were superior."

Interestingly enough, Jonathan Coxon worked for William Bromley Sr. at the time of this development and subsequently replaced him as Superintendent of Ott & Brewer when Bromley Sr. left to go to the Willets Manufacturing Company, a pottery competitor. And Coxon met Walter Lenox at Ott & Brewer, where Lenox was the Art Director. When they formed The Ceramic Art Company in 1889, Coxon and Lenox had learned well from the two Bromley masters and were able to make an immediate success of their new company.

The first companies making Belleek in Trenton used the word Belleek in their marks on the porcelain. That term or designation was continued by the later companies that made a similar type of porcelain. To the manufacturers, the word Belleek identified a particular type of porcelain, not merely a town in Ireland where a pottery was located. The use of the word began as an attempt to tell the public that the porcelain was the same or as good as the Irish porcelain.

At that particular time in history, Americans were quite prejudiced against most American-made products including local pottery and porcelain. Most buyers thought quality ware could only be made in Europe. The American Belleek companies did not try to imitate or copy the trademark used by the Irish factory, which has remained essentially the same with slight variations since the early 1860s. Ward Konkle reported, "the Coxon Company paid a royalty to the Irish Belleek Company for the use of the term Belleek. The same was true for the Morgan Belleek Company of Canton, Ohio, and for The Ceramic Art Company of Trenton."

In *American Belleek*, Mary Frank Gaston gives the most detailed and articulate description of the American Belleek era. According to Gaston,

> *The American companies were not trying to trick Americans into thinking their porcelain was made in Ireland. In fact, Ott & Brewer used Trenton and New Jersey in one of their Belleek marks. The early American Belleek manufacturers wanted above all to prove that quality porcelain could be made in America as well as in Europe. They were ultimately successful in that goal because the porcelain made by these several companies during the American Belleek era is still considered to be the finest work of the American porcelain industry and ranks on par with Europe porcelain made during that same time.*
>
> *The American Belleek era was relatively short-lived lasting only from 1883 to about 1930 — less than 50 years. The total number of companies involved in making American Belleek were fewer than twenty during that time, including firms in both Trenton, New Jersey and Ohio. Most of the companies were in business for only a few years; in fact, only five were in operation for more than ten years and only one, Lenox, Inc., is in business today. Two major factors brought about the downfall of the companies and the end of what can be called the American Belleek Era. First and foremost was the economic factor. Porcelain was expensive to produce; and, thus, expensive to purchase. The second factor related to the financial crisis in the United States during the 1890s that took its toll on some of the earlier companies; and the stock market crash in 1929 and the beginning of the Depression in 1930 that adversely affected the later firms.*

AMERICAN BELLEEK

From the early 1880s until about 1930, several American potteries manufactured a special type of porcelain that they called Belleek. The American Belleek companies are as follows:

Courtesy of Mary Frank Gaston, *American Belleek*

American Art China Co.,
(Trenton, New Jersey)

American Belleek Company,
(Trenton, New Jersey)

Belleek,
(company location unknown)

Ceramic Art Company,
(Trenton, New Jersey)

Columbian Art Pottery Co.,
(Trenton, New Jersey)

Cook Pottery Company,
(Trenton, New Jersey)

Coxon Belleek,
(Wooster, Ohio)

Gordon Belleek,
(company location unknown)

Knowles, Taylor & Knowles,
(East Liverpool, Ohio)

Lenox, Inc.,
(Trenton, New Jersey)

Morgan Belleek China Co.,
(Canton, Ohio)

Ott & Brewer,
(Trenton, New Jersey)

Perlee, Inc.,
(Trenton, New Jersey)

Willets Manufacturing Co.,
(Trenton, New Jersey)

SOURCES:

⫽ Capital Entertainment, July 17, 1992: "Antiques" by Nadja Maril

⫽ Ward and Dorothy Konkle

⫽ *American Belleek* by Mary Frank Gaston, published in 1984 by Collector Books, Paducah, Kentucky 42001.

Walter Lenox & Jonathan Coxon Sr.

A partnership of quality and its influence on the Coxon Belleek Company

The working lives of Jonathan Coxon Sr. and Walter Lenox crossed paths inside the same business for less than ten years, but their combined impact on the pottery, ceramics and china industry was felt for decades. Jonathan Coxon Sr. worked for a myriad of companies, always in the production and manufacturing end of the business. All six of his sons continued to work in the industry well into the 1900s. Walter Lenox, who also worked for several companies, may have been the person with the single largest impact on the design and artistry of china and porcelain in the history of the industry in the United States. Lenox and Coxon worked together for a few years for Ott & Brewer in the early 1880s, but during this short time together, it is clear that they must have developed sufficient respect and regard for each other that they began plans to start a business together. In 1889, and for a brief period of seven years, these two giants of the industry combined forces and expertise by forming The Ceramic Art Company, which eventually evolved into Lenox China. Mr. Lenox brought the artistic vision and Mr. Coxon brought the manufacturing expertise.

Their time in working together at Ott & Brewer was a critical springboard for both men. In 1889, an exhibition of pottery and glassware was held in Philadelphia, and the Ott and Brewer display received considerable attention. In the *Daily True American*, the reporter noted that tremendous advancements had occurred in the industry, much attributed to Ott & Brewer, "... they have advanced with steady progression to the enviable position of leaders in the fine art of pottery in this country, and have placed themselves on the front rank of all the potters of the world. It is true that their first efforts were duplicates of the famous Irish Belleek, but a glance at their display will convince anyone at all acquainted with the art that they have improved and beautified this class of goods to a wonderful extent."

He goes on to say, "Unquestionably, during this period Ott & Brewer was one of the more exciting places of employment on the Trenton pottery scene. It is no surprise, therefore, that from the ranks of Ott & Brewer came many who were destined to make important contributions at other potteries or on their own. The best known of all Trenton potteries, Lenox China Co., is also a direct offshoot of this company. The founders, Jonathan Coxon and Walter Lenox, received much of their critical training and experience while at Ott & Brewer."

The Ceramic Art Company was founded on May 16, 1889 by Walter S. Lenox, Jonathan Coxon Sr., William S. Hancock and Joseph Rice, with Hancock and Rice providing financial backing and Coxon and Lenox providing financial backing as well as operational expertise. Coxon and Lenox held the majority of the shares.

Coxon, as its President, was in charge of the overall operation with particular attention to manufacture of the porcelain body and general production management. David Goldberg in his monograph *Preliminary Notes on the Pioneer Potters and Potteries of Trenton, New Jersey* writes "Jonathan Coxon was a knowledgeable potter in his own right by virtue of his background and experience with his uncle, Charles Coxon. At Mercer Pottery he held the position of Superintendent and assumed similar responsibilities at Ott & Brewer. There is little doubt that the insights that he learned from the Bromleys [William Sr. and William Jr.] reshaped his notions of the pottery business and charted the course that would be followed by The Ceramic Art Company which he and Lenox founded in 1889."

From its very inception, The Ceramic Art Company committed itself to the production of fine Belleek china and decorative and artistic pieces of the highest quality. Lenox, with his artistic background handled the design of the wares and management of

the decorating department, served as Secretary and Treasurer of the Company.

Hancock owned Crescent Pottery, which merged in 1892 with four other potteries, all making primarily sanitary goods, into Trenton Potteries Company. He had many other financial interests included banking, insurance and philanthropy. He helped to found Mercer Hospital, organized the Trenton Opera House and the Trent Theater. He also held the position of State Controller. Coxon worked for Hancock when he owned Crescent Pottery and likely persuaded Hancock to invest in this new company. Hancock was the largest cash investor of the four men when the company was formed.

Rice was a merchant tailor, clothier and one of Trenton's most highly respected citizens. Born in 1834 in Baden, Germany, he established his clothing business in Trenton in the 1850s. He was a member of the Police Board of Commissioners beginning in 1889, and played a prominent role in the affairs of Mechanic's National Bank from 1891 until his death in 1913.

With this highly competent group of practical and financial men formally organized, The Ceramic Art Company was launched with the capitalization of $7,000.00 with Lenox and Coxon holding the largest shares.

In the book entitled *Lenox China: Celebrating a Century of Quality: 1889 through 1989*, Ellen Paul Denker, states "from 1889 to 1905, The Ceramic Art Company defined the perfection of porcelain also called china as a fine art. This small studio made delicately molded Belleek china exquisitely hand decorated with figures and flowers by artists from America and Europe."

In May 1896, the corporation underwent some big changes. Coxon retired from an operational role in the company and apparently from the pottery business as well, to devote his time to the Trenton parks. He was nearly sixty years of age and had given most of those years to pottery. His retirement from the company was followed by resignation from the board of directors, and the transfer of his thirty-four shares of stock to Lenox.

Rice also withdrew from the company and assigned his single share of stock to Harry Brown, who had been keeping the company's books. Hancock remained a director and vital member of the organization until his death in 1915. Lenox became the President and Treasurer, while Brown was elected Secretary. Lenox continued the quality of product into the 1900s and in 1906 changed the name of The Ceramic Art Company to Lenox China. Lenox China continued to grow and over the years became the largest china company in the United States. Lenox China remains in business today.

Did this seven-year partnership between Lenox and Coxon and their creation of The Ceramic Art Company and its evolution into Lenox China impact the decision to start the Coxon Belleek Company in 1925? The answer is clearly yes. Coxon and Lenox maintained a positive relationship over the years because when Coxon died, one of the few flower arrangements mentioned in his obituary came from Walter Lenox. As we examine the history of the Lenox Company, it is clear the Coxon family followed its fortunes very closely. Key decisions made by the Lenox Company over the years were adapted and even copied by the Coxon Belleek Company in its business plan. The similarities are multifold, and include the development and use of the Belleek formula, quality of product, use of distributors, sales territories, decorating techniques, use of decals combined with hand painting, and staff configuration. However, there is clear divergence between The Ceramic Arts Company/Lenox and Coxon Belleek, especially with marketing and design trends. If Coxon Belleek had followed the example of Lenox in these areas, their potential for long-term success could have been vastly improved.

Jonathan Coxon had a history and commitment to high quality. Denker states, "The Ceramic Art Company was ready to exhibit its first wares, which were described as pretty, original, artistic, beautiful, elegant, and entirely fresh in design. The company's first advertisement stressed the original shapes, the superb styles of the decorated goods, and the pure white fabric especially adapted to the wants of amateur decorators. Reporters were continually impressed with the high quality of work being produced by such a small operation." Jonathan Coxon was responsible for the manufacturing process at The Ceramic Arts Company, but, before and after he left the company, he recognized that the designs by The Ceramic Arts Company and, subsequently, Lenox China anchored the success of selling the product and he surely imparted this knowledge to his sons. Coxon Belleek also developed the ability to respond to the customer's needs. They were the only company that allowed for custom orders as a standard business option. A customer could actually order a unique, one-of-a-kind set of china, choosing the pattern, colors, and bands with or without gold or silver. This custom work, although certainly more expensive, gave them an advantage over their competitors until the Depression negatively impacted the customer's ability to purchase much of the fine china made in America and Europe.

From 1889–1896, both Coxon and Lenox developed and perfected their unique Belleek process, which contributed greatly to the sale of the product as well. Similarly, in 1925, Coxon Belleek developed a Belleek product that was translucent, strong and beautiful from the moment the first product was sold. This was no accident because the Coxon sons had access to the Belleek formula used by their father and Lenox in The Ceramic Arts Company venture. In addition, Coxon Belleek developed a high quality translucent glaze using a wide array of colors. Again, the touchstone with The Ceramic Art Company and

Lenox China was evident. Talking about Lenox China, a reviewer for Pottery and Glass in 1908 declared "The superb quality and translucency of the Lenox china, the perfection of detail in designing and modeling, the richness of gilding and inexhaustible pallet of hard-fired colors apply to beautifully transparent and luscious glaze, place it practically in a class by itself and have made it one of the most renowned porcelains in the world. Delicate flower designs are usually preferred for the plates. The coffee sets are in graceful antique shapes with decoration to match." If this reviewer had been writing in 1925–31, he would have been describing Coxon Belleek. Decker says, "Although some of the earliest work produced by the companies' craftsmen and artists were similar to the Trenton Belleek products of the 1880s, Lenox altered the definition of art porcelain in America by introducing a new look, the raised gold and silver decorations in the ascetic style of the earlier period were replaced by highly finished figure and flower painting framed by colored backgrounds, richly ornamented with raised gold and contrasting enamel decorations." Although Coxon Belleek did much less hand-painting than was done by The Ceramic Arts Company/Lenox in the late 1800s and early 1900s, their flowered designs, wide array of colors, use of gold and silver, and glaze were strikingly similar.

Denker states, "By January 1892, The Ceramic Art Company also employed at least one traveling representative and in 1894, the company proposed to send samples to dealers who were unable to inspect the line in person." This is the exact business plan utilized by Coxon Belleek. It is very illuminating that Coxon Belleek had developed a business relationship with a large number of jewelers and department stores throughout the country from the outset of their operation. This was not coincidental. Their father taught them this model and the name "Coxon," and its identification with high quality china, quickly connected with well-established jewelry stores all over the country.

Denker also says,

The way in which Ceramic Art Company was organized in both staff and space was in sharp contrast to the operations of most other American concerns. It is more like the studio of an artist than the real live working pottery that it is, noted one reporter, and I'm not sure but that the application of studio would fit it much more gracefully than the more common word factory. Lenox's desire to employ a small, highly trained staff to concentrate on one type of product, art porcelain, and to offer the product as the highest form of the potters and painters arts, suggested the spirit of The Ceramic Art Company, and was revolutionary, even if the style of the product was conservative.

Coxon Belleek was a blend of an art studio and a china factory. It was one of the few china companies that manufactured one-of-a-kind unique sets of china for individual customers. Many of their designs have similarities, but there are hundreds of unique china patterns. In addition, patterns were hand-painted and the use of gold and silver was evidenced on many of the patterns. As a result, Coxon Belleek utilized a staffing pattern very similar to what occurred with The Ceramic Arts Company/Lenox.

The Ceramic Arts Company/Lenox "also employed at least two salesmen to promote its wares across the country. The accounts listed in the 1903 ledger identified W.H. Bush and George W. Milligan, who maintained both sample and commission accounts with the company. Milligan had Chicago and west for his territory, while Bush handled New England." Although the names of the sales representatives are unknown, Coxon Belleek utilized a similar sales model and had jewelers and department stores throughout the country selling their china.

Decker says,

The next major development in the transition of the firm from an art studio to a tableware producer occurred in 1917 when Lenox's first lithograph pattern was introduced. Decal decoration (called decalomania at the time) is printed lithographically in full color on a film conveyed by a paper backing. When the paper is soaked in water, the decal can be slipped away from it and onto the surface of a plate for fixing in the fire. Filling in additional color is not required, although many Lenox decal designs have been enhanced with raised enamels. With decals, Lenox could offer high quality decorated tableware to a larger audience and thereby increase sales. The earlier use of printed and filled patterns had resulted in some audience expansion because wares could be produced at a lower price than designs painted entirely by hand. The pattern filling still required painters albeit having somewhat less skill than the painters of china in the late 1800s and early 1900s. The use of decals on the other hand eliminated the need for painters when color was wanted. In addition to reducing the cost of producing tableware, decals also virtually guaranteed color consistency and presented the consumer with a recognizable product.

Lenox started the widespread use of decals, and Coxon Belleek followed this trend. Coxon Belleek used decals that were purchased from the Palm Fechteler Company of New York and Florida. Coxon Belleek had only two pattern names: Iota and Boulevard. Instead, the individual decal number assigned by the Palm Fechteler Company identified each one of the hundreds of individual patterns.

However, there were significant differences in advertising and marketing strategies between Ceramic Art Company/Lenox China and Coxon Belleek. Decker states, "In May 1891, the pending publication of Ceramic Art Pottery's first catalog was announced. The catalog facilitated direct sale to many retailers and in 1892, jewelers were noted as the principal retail outlets in other cities." Regarding Lenox, Denker states,

Walter Scott Lenox maintained an active role in this merchandising. In 1908 and 1909, the company produced a group of small format booklets that included an instruction manual, china colors and fire, and four additional catalogs that offered a variety of forms in several categories. Tea, coffee, mocha and chocolate sets, tankard steins, jugs, loving cups, punch bowls and smoking sets, vases and tableware, desk and toilet articles.

A small but elegant booklet on Lenox china dinnerware was also published in 1908. This catalog illustrated a few of the shapes available and suggested various types of decorations that could be ordered, including fish and fowl designs, monogramming, and gold edgings.

Lenox China also advertised in the trade magazines and women's magazines, and published a catalog to help promote their wares and that offered special forms or articles for private parties who may desire to control an exclusive and uncommon line. This undoubtedly applied to retailers who wanted to offer an exclusive line of tea or coffee pieces or a manufacturer that wished to collaborate with the company on a particular offering, and organizations that needed souvenirs for a special event.

There is scant evidence that Coxon Belleek did any advertising in journals, magazines or newspapers, although with the quality of their product, it would not have been difficult to accomplish. In addition, there is no evidence of handbooks, brochures, books or any other form of publication similar to that accomplished by Walter Lenox. Marketing and advertising were barely utilized by the Coxon Belleek Company. Would a comprehensive marketing strategy have helped Coxon Belleek stay afloat? The reality may well be that, without marketing and advertising, Coxon Belleek was doomed to failure, even taking into account the emergence of the depression.

Presidential china, up until 1918, had always been made in France, China, or England. President Wilson had strong ties to New Jersey and when he became President, he looked to Lenox China for the White House as an especially loyal and patriotic decision. "The commission went to Lenox for an order of 1,700 pieces, estimated to cost $11,251.60, and was placed on March 30, 1918, and delivered to the White House in several shipments between August and November. Although the praise and trade papers that continued for Lenox wares did not differ materially from the favorable comments that had followed the company since its inception as The Ceramic Art Company, the weight of the Presidential commission gave the words more meaning. Commentators had declared for years that Walter Lenox's achievements one after another proved that American fine china was as good as European, but this new distinction seems finally to have secured the company's future reputation." Coxon Belleek wished to secure a similar reputation. There actually was an article in the Wooster *Daily Record* about a set of china sent to the White House. Regretfully, there is no evidence that this actually happened. A records check with the White House, and with the Hoover Museum, has no record of the purchase of, or receipt of, Coxon Belleek china. This could have been more of a hope than an actuality. Or unsolicited, Coxon Belleek could have just prepared a special set of china for the White House. Again, this demonstrates how much respect the business practices of the Lenox China Company held with the Coxon sons and how much they wished to gain the same acclaim from the general public.

Yes, it is clear that Coxon Belleek looked closely toward Lenox China for its business model. In many ways, they replicated the quality of the product, the ways of doing business, and the knowledge of the industry. However, the advent of the Depression was a major blow, and a lack of a marketing vision and advertising campaign a crucial factor in the business failure.

This could have been a sample of the "White House" china.

SOURCES:

/// *Lenox China: Celebrating a Century of Quality: 1889 through 1989*, by Ellen Paul Denker

/// *Preliminary Notes on the Pioneer Potters and Potteries of Trenton New Jersey, the First Thirty Years 1852–1882 (And Beyond)*, David J. Goldberg c. 1983 Trenton, New Jersey

/// Ward and Dorothy Konkle

THE PARTNERS AND STARTING THE BUSINESS IN WOOSTER

Of all the American Belleek potteries trying to get established over the years, Coxon Belleek should have been the most likely one to succeed. Certainly the firm had all the ingredients for success. Two of the founders, J. Fred and Edward Coxon, were sons of Jonathan Coxon Sr. and the third Coxon founder, Edward Jr., was the grandson of Jonathan. The two Coxon sons had worked with Jonathan Sr. and were in possession of the Belleek formula obtained from workers brought to America from Belleek, Ireland. All three partners brought much knowledge and experience to the new enterprise.

The first Coxon to move to the Wooster area was J. Frederick Coxon. Fred, the youngest son of Jonathan Sr., worked for his father and then went from Trenton, New Jersey to Kokomo, Indiana in the late 1800s where he worked for his two older brothers, William and Edward at the Great Western Pottery Company that made sanitary porcelain products. In 1900, after learning the business, he was named the Superintendent of the Tiffin, Ohio branch of Great Western Pottery at the age of twenty-one. In 1913–14, Fred was one of three incorporators of the Wooster China Company along with Fred Bell and Al Harrison. They bought the defunct Fredericksburg Pottery Company plant in Fredericksburg, Ohio and the Wooster China Company began making bathroom fixtures. Fred remained in Tiffin until 1916 when he moved to Wooster. It is unknown when he resigned from the Great Western Pottery Company, what his position was with the Wooster China Company, how long he stayed with the company, or how much he invested and profited.

Interestingly enough, an article from *The Times Democrat* in Lima, Ohio, August 17, 1916 detailing Ohio Incorporations stated that the Wooster Pottery Company of Fredericksburg, Ohio increased their share subscription from $5,000.00 to $7,000.00. This was around the time that Fred moved to Wooster and also started the Fredericksburg Pottery Company. Was this a name change for the same company or was this another pottery company?

Then, in 1919, the *City Directory of Wooster and Bloomington* described J. Frederick Coxon as affiliated with the Wooster Sanitary Manufacturing Company. The records are unclear if this represented another name change for the Fredericksburg company, or whether a separate company located in Wooster existed.

In 1921, the Wooster China Company bought an iron and enamel plant in Salem, Ohio and changed its name to the National Sanitary Company. In 1923, the National Sanitary Company bought a sanitary products plant in Clarksburg, West Virginia. In 1927, the Elger Manufacturing Company bought all of the National Sanitary Company's plants. It obviously was a very successful enterprise, which grew significantly in the decade of business.

The relationship between the Wooster China Company, the Wooster Pottery Company, the Wooster Sanitary Manufacturing Company, and the National Sanitary Company is unclear. The level of J. Frederick Coxon's involvement with these companies is also unclear. However, it is clear that Fred brought much knowledge of the china industry into play in his early years in Wooster. It is also clear that Fred was a multi-tasking entrepreneur and that he made a healthy profit through these businesses.

Edward T., J. Fred's older brother by ten years, brought extensive experience in the china and pottery industry. Early in his career, he worked for his father, Jonathan Sr. in The Ceramic Art Company in Trenton and then moved soon after 1893 to Kokomo, Indiana, after his older brother W.G. Coxon incorporated the Great Western Pottery Company. An article in the *Kokomo Journal* in 1953 shares the beginning of the involvement of Coxons in the Great Western Pottery Company.

The Great Western Pottery Company started production in 1893. Three Kokomo citizens, A.B. Conradt, his son, A.V. Conradt, and W.G. Coxon, organized the company. Great Western expanded in 1899 with the purchase of the Brewer Pottery Company of Tiffin, Ohio. The Brewer Company was manufacturer of dinnerware and other general pottery items. But after the purchase, production of Tiffin was changed to sanitary ware. When the plant started production, it had approximately fifty employees. It grew and expanded, changed ownership and methods and equipment, and employed over two hundred and fifty. It was one of the largest potteries in Indiana, and manufactured a wide variety of vitreous plumbing fixtures. The American Standard Plant occupied a thirteen-acre

tract. Its buildings covered more than four acres with over 330,000 square feet under roof. From the beginning of operations, the Kokomo plant manufactured only sanitary wares, such as water closets. During the years that followed, additional types of water closets were made at both plants.

Edward T. Coxon was ten years younger than W.G. Coxon and came to work in management positions for the company in the early 1890s. Then J. Fred, ten years younger than Edward T., came to Kokomo in the late 1890s. He worked in Kokomo and then, in 1900, was named the plant manager for the company at the Tiffin branch of Great Western at the age of twenty-one.

John Frederick "J. Fred" Coxon

Edward T. was very successful prior to moving to Wooster. This is indicated through an article in the Kokomo Tribune, entitled "Several Sales Are Reported By Realty Men," "One of the largest transactions of the week involved property valued at approximately $17,000.00 and was negotiated by Joe Jay. Through the negotiations, Harrison Mills, Manager of the Kingston Drugstore, traded his property at 1226 North Indiana Avenue for a seven-room modern house at 920 West Mulberry Street owned by E.T. Coxon. Mr. Coxon, with his son, Ed B. Coxon, and their families, has moved to Wooster, Ohio, where they own and operate the Belleek China Company factory." Edward came to Wooster a wealthy man.

Much less is known about Edward B., son of Edward T. Edward B. also worked with the Great Western Pottery Company in Kokomo with his father and three uncles (William, Theodore and J. Frederick). While there, he worked in various plant management positions before moving to Wooster.

In 1925–26, Edward T. Coxon and Edward's son, Edward B., joined Fred in Wooster to start Coxon Belleek. Edward T. brought much experience in the pottery industry from the early 1890s–1918 and was even more experienced in the china industry than was his younger brother Fred. Edward also brought with him his personal financial backing because of his success in Kokomo. This was combined with J. Fred's financial success and business expertise gained from his experience in Tiffin, Fredericksburg and Wooster.

When the Coxon Belleek Company was dissolved in late 1931, it had over $220,000 of unsecured debt, which was the equivalent of $2,647,035 in 2007. The investors and their respective shares are unknown, but the two Edwards and Fred were likely the major contributors in capitalizing the company. On January 3, 1927, the Coxons bought a one-acre plot of land on East Bowman Street in Wooster from the Wooster Board of Trade. There was one small building there and the Coxons built an addition to it for the main part of their factory.

Vivian Coxon (wife of J. Fred)

Coxon Belleek would never have been able to start so quickly without the working knowledge of the crucial Belleek formula provided through Jonathan Coxon Sr. From the very first, the quality of Coxon Belleek China matched that of Irish Belleek. The formula included detailed knowledge of a myriad of products and the unique synergy between these products when mixed.

It took knowledge and money to build the pottery, hire skilled men for the operation, and train the decorators. John I. Bahl, an artist and decorator who had been trained at the Knowles, Taylor & Knowles Company at East Liverpool started with Coxon Belleek and when the company failed in the early 1930s Bahl was hired by the American Chinaware Company at their Morgan Belleek plant in Canton until they soon failed. Another artist, Lewis Crosier, was with Coxon Belleek Company for several years. At the peak of its production, Coxon Belleek employed about seventy-five workers.

Coxon Belleek operated two large kilns and several smaller ones, all fired by gas. One of the reasons for the consistently high quality of Coxon Belleek was the fact that the East Ohio Gas Company stationed one of their men at the pottery to monitor gas pressure, thereby insuring proper firing. In contrast, Coxon Belleek's Ohio rival, Morgan Belleek of Canton, had coal-fired kilns, which were harder to control, a factor, some say, that led to their demise.

Very quickly, the company had accounts with some of the largest and most prestigious department and jewelry stores throughout the country. This was not coincidental. This was due to the long-term relationships and the high credibility built by the Coxon family over many years in the china and pottery industry since the late 1800s. The buyers and owners of these stores were dealing with a known entity: the Coxon family. The relationships were already cemented when they started their new enterprise.

J. Fred, Edward T., and Edward B. formed a knowledgeable and financially sound triumvirate. With the Coxon reputation, Coxon expertise, Coxon money and Coxon entrepreneurial spirit, the future of the Coxon Belleek China Company looked bright.

SOURCES:

/// Ward and Dorothy Konkle

/// "World's Finest China is Produced in Wooster," *The Daily Record*, Wooster Ohio.

/// *Coxon Fine China Name*, Published by Ovington's New York and Chicago.

/// *The History of the Fredericksburg, Ohio Potteries and Reference Guide*, Bill Ports, 2007.

/// *Kokomo Journal*, Thursday, December 3, 1953: "Pottery Observes 60th Anniversary: Vast Expansion Over Period Is Revealed."

Outlets of Jewelry and Department Stores

Coxon Belleek china was sold in high quality jewelry stores and department stores in most of the major cities in the country. The number of outlets found to date is thirty-seven, located in twenty-five cities and one foreign country (Paris, France). Undoubtedly, there were many more. Outlets were located in seventeen States in all regions of the country (Northeast-ten; Southeast-one; South-one; West-two; and Midwest-eleven). The outlets found to date printed under the Coxon Belleek logo are as follows, alphabetically according to outlet:

B. Altman & Company, Paris and New York

L. Bamberger & Company, Newark, NJ

Bromberg Galleries, Birmingham, AL

Burley & Company, Chicago, IL

The Cowell & Hubbard Company,
Cleveland, OH

Corrigan, Inc., Jewelers, Houston, TX

The Dayton Company, Minneapolis, MN

Dulany Vornay Co., Baltimore, MD

Arthur A. Everts Company, Jewelers,
Dallas, TX

Glass and Queensware Co., St. Louis, MO

S.&G. Gump Co., San Francisco, CA

Charles Hall, Inc., Springfield, MA

The William Hintershield Company,
Columbus, OH

Hochschild, Kohn & Co., Baltimore, MD

J.L. Hudson Company, Detroit, MI

made expressly for T. M. James & Sons China
Company, Kansas City, MO

The F&R Lazarus & Company, Columbus, OH

The Lewis & Nesblett Co., Cincinnati, OH

Marks & Fuller, Inc., Rochester, NY

Frank Mersomede Company, Cincinnati, OH

Edwin W. Neimand, Jeweler, Davenport, IA

F.S. Nash & Company, Pasadena, CA

Omaha Crockery Co., Omaha, NE

Ovington's, Newark and Chicago

Ovington's , New York and Chicago

Ovington's, New York

Perkins, Hartford, CT

A .J. Powell & Co., Inc., Boston, MA

The D.M. Reed Company,
Bridgeport, CT

Rothschild Kohn & Company,
Baltimore, MD

St. Louis Glass & Queensware Company,
St. Louis, MO

Schunemans & Mannheimers,
St. Paul, MN

The Shepard Company, Providence, RI

Shibley & Hudson, Wooster, OH

Unique Marks with Coxon Belleek Logo

Made expressly for John Wannemaker,
New York, New York

Made expressly for John Wannemaker,
Philadelphia, Pennsylvania

Made Expressly for Dr. and Mrs. A.R. Spindler

"w" inside shield

"lion"

"a" inside shield

Coxon Belleek (handwritten in block letters,
upper and lower case)

OPERATIONS AND THE ELUSIVE NUMBERING SYSTEM

How good was Coxon Belleek china? An article from the Wooster *Daily Record* in the late 1920s addresses the quality of the Coxon Belleek product and compares it to European and American competition.

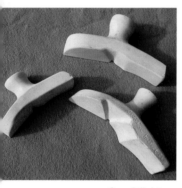

Coxon Belleek jiggers

In recent tests conducted by the United States government, Coxon china stood at the very top of the wares investigated, including all the better foreign products. These tests were for chipping, crazing, or checking, and in them, the Wooster ware was matched with other chinas of equal or heavier weights. Coxon china produced through a secret process from feldspar and numerous clays has a creamy body that is translucent. English china, the famous bone china, has a blue-white body. Displays on white linen tablecloths show the Wooster product decidedly superior and that it offers a contrast to the background. It lends itself admirably to decoration and these factors, together with its hardness—it is almost unbreakable—make it a real leader. The bugaboo of the imported myth is the chief obstacle in the path of its more rapid acceptance in the higher quality markets in the land. The larger American potteries for many years have been manufacturing a product whose standard was inferior to the best-imported grades. Consequently, buyers from homes where the cost of china counted little in comparison to quality, gave American ware no consideration. They were convinced that foreign ware was superior. Now with Coxon china on the market, this myth has been exploded, but it requires a long time to drive that* fact home to the folks who can afford the excellent ware that is made in Wooster. In [these] recent tests conducted by the United States government, Coxon china stood at the very top of the wares investigated, including all of the better foreign products. The government test has greatly heartened the management of the Wooster plant. It has demonstrated what they have known for many years—that Coxon china has no superior anywhere.*

Granted, a Wooster newspaper will have a certain bias in favor of a local business, but the government tests confirm their opinion of the quality of the product. How was Coxon Belleek china made? Ward Konkle, the first curator of the Coxon Belleek collection at the Wayne County Historical Society, interviewed several former workers at the plant prior to their deaths. His interviews yielded crucial information about the production process. Mr. Robert Hunter, one of the Coxon Belleek jigger men, talked about the production process as follows:

China items, such as teapots, pitchers, and sugar molds were made by using molds. A Mr. Crosier, who lived on North Grant Street, was a mold maker. The bulk of the Coxon output, however, consisted of dinnerware, and those items were made by means of an old reliable potter's wheel, a flat mold, and the use of a jigger. The ground clay used to make the dinnerware was called slip, and had a consistency of thick soup. It was kept in a large tank and constantly agitated to keep it ready for use. The

*craftsman who used the jigger was known as a jigger man,
and that was the role that I [Mr. Hunter] had at Coxon.
After being formed, the pieces of dinnerware were placed
in a kiln where a temperature of about 2,000 degrees
Fahrenheit was maintained for the firing. The time
and temperature of the firing were very critical. Coxon
used gas as the fuel for heating the kiln and because
the gas pressure at the plant varied, the East Ohio Gas
Company quite frequently stationed one of their experts
at the Coxon plant to make sure a steady flow of gas was
delivered to the firing chamber. When one of the big kilns
was fully loaded, a temperature change could mean the
loss of up to $20,000 worth of dinnerware. During this
first firing, the particles and the clay mix became fused
together and hardened like porcelain. When the pieces
came out, they were called bisque, which had to be sanded
down, buffed and inspected to be sure they measured up
to a standard quality. One of the ways they tested a piece
was to hold it up to a light to determine if you could see
your fingers through the piece. Those that didn't pass the
test were destroyed.*

*Next, the bisque was dipped in the glazing solution and
then put back into the kiln for a second firing. This is the
way it looked when it came from the second firing, which
is a plain piece. The ware was then ready for decorating.
Basic decorating was done by means of a paper transfer
or decal process, and this was added to and touched up
where necessary by skilled artists. Some of the patterns
appear to be hand decorated. Next, the ware was again
dipped in the glaze solution and returned to the kiln for
the third firing, after which it was considered a finished
product, except for the adding of the gold striping.*

Mrs. Robert Hunter (wife of Robert), an inspector for Coxon Belleek, added, "Coxon shipped out a lot of plain ware and it was sold either 'as is' or else decorated by the store or company that bought it. Some of the larger stores in New York, Philadelphia and Chicago had Coxon put their own firm name on the dinnerware during the decorating process." One often hears people talk about having seconds, but she questions this. Mrs. Hunter, as an inspector, recalled standing at the back door throwing out the seconds.

She said, "One of the ways you can tell Belleek-

Coxon Belleek "jigger man" Robert Hunter

type china is to hold a piece up to the light and you can actually see your fingers through the piece." Inspectors would break and discard any piece of Coxon Belleek that did not have this translucent quality. The Coxons instantly had to pay a royalty to the Irish company for the use of the term Belleek.

Mr. Konkle went on to report, "the Coxon Company paid a royalty to the Irish Belleek Company for the use of the term Belleek. The same was true for the Morgan Belleek Company of Canton, Ohio, and for The Ceramic Art Company of Trenton. The number of employees at the Coxon pottery varied from fifty to seventy-five, depending upon the flow of business. About a dozen of these were artists, two of whom were highly skilled artists from the east."

Coxon Belleek china was very colorful. The plate illustrated on the next page shows certain colors from the bottom left and moving clockwise, emery melon green, second color: emery peacock green, number

2382, third color: emery chrome green, number 2392, fourth color: sneyd plum, number 310, fifth color: sneyd blue, number 483-A, sixth color: sneyd plum, number 315, seventh color: sneyd blue, number 1176, eighth color: emery green, ninth color: emery apple green, number 1838, tenth color: emery chrome green, number 173, eleventh color: BFD Arlington green, twelfth color: GFD Persian red, number 207, and thirteenth color: emery azure blue, number 822.

Coxon Belleek named only two of their patterns; Iota and Boulevard. Iota was named for the personal office secretary of Fred Coxon. However, there are hundreds of patterns, some unmarked and many marked with a series of numbers and letters. For years, the system of marking the patterns was unknown. No sales manuals, catalogs or company documents have been found.

In the 1996 exhibit of Coxon Belleek at the Wayne County Historical Society, it was determined that the last capital letter in the numbering series represented the color of the wide band in the pattern. For exam-

ple, "Y" stood for yellow, "M" stood for maroon, "G" stood for green, etc. In the research for this book, the records of the Coxon Belleek bankruptcy were examined. One of the creditors was the Palm & Fechteler Company. Further research at the New York Historical Society yielded information about this company as well as an affiliate, the Palm Brothers Company. Both were decal companies and based in New York City and Florida. When examining their sales brochures, each decal pattern was numbered, and these numbers corresponded to the individual decal pattern on the individual Coxon Belleek patterns. The mystery was solved!

The use of decals in the china industry is actually called decalcomania. It is an art or process of transferring designs from specially prepared paper to china, glass, marble, etc., and permanently fixing them thereto.

The Palm Company said that

...a form of decalcomania started in the 1300s [when] art teachers used transfers and instant art workshops for

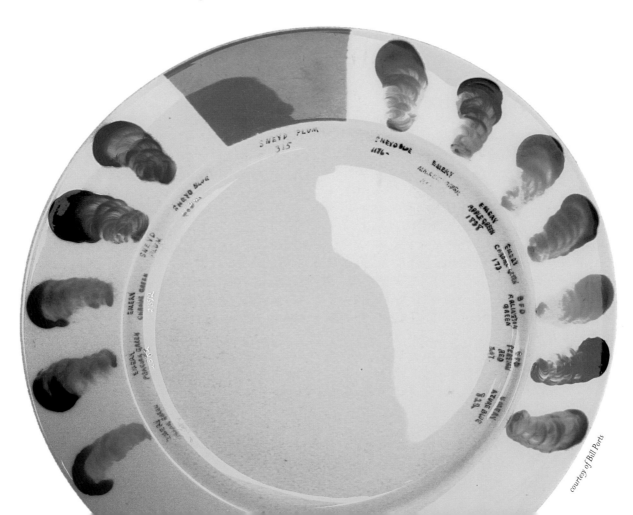

the gentry. Then, in 1800, a new method of printing was invented. Lithographers drew on a smooth stone with a grease crayon and then etched the exposed stone with an acid. To print, they dampened the stone with water and rolled oil-based colors over it. The oily ink was repelled by the water and only stuck to the oily crayon image. Press a sheet of paper against the stone and a very detailed print could be pulled. The next step came by using paper coated with an extra heavy sized layer, printing on the side with oil colors and thus creating an image that can be transferred off the paper by re-dissolving the glue paper.

The directions for using mineral transfers used in the 20s and later are fairly simple:

- *Spread varnish with brush over the space to be occupied by the transfer*
- *See that each and every spot is covered but do not use too much or transfer will blister in the fire*
- *Let the varnish get tacky before applying transfer*
- *Place the transfer face downward on the china, wetting it with a damp sponge*
- *Press firmly so that the transfer will adhere well to the china; peel the paper carefully from the film*
- *When the paper is removed, wash the transfer over thoroughly with a wet sponge*
- *Pat with damp chamois very carefully and let it stand for twenty-four hours to dry before tiring*
- *With duplex transfers, pressing with damp sponge is all that's necessary*

Palm Brothers made to order all kinds of transfers, trademarks, and special designs for decorating of china, porcelain, earthenware, glass, enamelware, wood, metal, silk, leather, cloth and rubber.

The godfather of the china industry was Walter Lenox. In his *The Proper Methods of Decorating and Firing China*, published in 1908, Mr. Lenox wrote chapters on "China Colors and Fire;" "How Our Colors Are Prepared and Applied;" "Dry Ground Laying;" "Application of Flat Gold;" "Raised Paste Work;" "Enamel Jewelry" and "The Firing of Belleek China." This publication was the bible of china making, and all subsequent manufacturers of fine china used Mr.

Lenox's guidelines for making their china, including Coxon Belleek. As with many of his innovations in the industry, the Coxons adhered closely to Mr. Lenox's principles and techniques in decorating and firing china.

In one respect, Coxon Belleek was truly unique in the china industry. The company chose a few patterns that were shown and sold as company patterns. However, a customer who wanted a unique, one-of-a-kind pattern could chose a pattern from the decal book provided by the Palm Companies. Customers were able to choose the decal, bands, and colors, probably with the assistance of trained individuals at the jewelry store or department store. Then, Coxon Belleek, armed with the final choice of the customer, with advice of their interior decorator or the jeweler, produced a set of china totally unique to individual taste. Because the customer chose the pattern, if a plate was broken, the customer could reorder the personalized pattern from the decal number originally chosen by the customer. Coxon Belleek produced hundreds of unique, one-of-a-kind china patterns, individually produced for the customer and never duplicated again.

This also answers the question of the evidence of duplicate decorations on china manufactured by many different companies. The companies were not infringing upon a design patent of another company. Instead, each company purchased decals from Palm & Fechteler, some of which were identical or very similar. Evidence of similar china patterns from Morgan Belleek, Syracuse China, Coxon Belleek, Lenox China and many others support the common choice of certain decals.

SOURCES:

/// *The New Illustrated Catalog and Price List of the Palm Brothers Company*, as well as archival material from the New York Historical Society about the same company.

/// *The Daily Record*, Tuesday, June 30, 1987, "Plenty of Collectors for Coxon Belleek".

/// Ward and Dorothy Konkle

DEMISE OF A QUALITY COMPANY

Business filing information from the State of Ohio for the Coxon Belleek China Company...

```
FILING TYPE:
DOMESTIC ARTICLES FOR PROFIT

FILING DATE:
DECEMBER 11, 1925

CANCELLED/UNABLE TO
DETERMINE/OLD INCOMPLETE
RECORDS, NOVEMBER 15, 1932.
```

Ward Konkle reports,

Late in 1930, hard times fell on the Coxon enterprise, not only because of the Depression, but also because of poor management. Records of the Wayne County Recorder's Office show that during 1930 and 1931, a number of liens were slapped on them. Most of these, however, were paid off. Eventually, the Great Depression finally spelled doom for the Coxon Belleek China Company in 1931. Some said their product was too high priced of a luxury for depression times, but on November 4, 1931, the Coxons sold their property back to the Wooster Board of Trade. The Coxon Corporation was dissolved in September 1932.

There were indications of money issues for the Coxon family in the late 20s. On August 6, 1927, the United Cigar Stores of America, Plaintiff, took Ed-

ward B. Coxon to court to recover a $700.00 judgment. Before it appeared in front of the judge, Mr. Coxon paid the bill. Again, on November 6, 1927, the same incident occurred. In U.S. Cigar Stores of America vs. Edward B. Coxon, Edward B. again paid $403.90 to the U.S. Cigar Stores of America before the case appeared before a judge. However, in 1929, the case of U.S. Cigar Stores of America vs. Edward B. Coxon was defaulted at $518.00, and no payment was made.

There was a bill from the Palm Fechteler Company, which had provided the decals for the china, starting April 1, 1929, with a $1,000 balance owed by Coxon Belleek. "On 3/24/1930, the Coxon Belleek China Company, Wooster, Ohio, served to E.T. Coxon, he being director of said Belleek china company, there being no President, Vice-President, or any higher active officer found in the county at any time of service.

Judgment by default: $570.43, plus costs. The debt continues all the way through to October 8, 1930, and the final amount owed was $559.25."

An indication of business decline was a huge ad that appeared in the March 7, 1930 edition of *The Daily Record*. The ad read as follows:

Special sale of Coxon Belleek china at the factory, East Bowman Street, open to the public March 6, 7, and 8. A limited number of patterns at reduced prices. A chance of a lifetime to secure for yourself and friends some of the world's finest dinnerware.

Then, in the Court of Common Pleas of Wayne County, Ohio on June 27, 1930, a case was brought to court entitled "Vivian K. Coxon vs. The Coxon Belleek China Company, A Corporation, Defendant." Vivian was the wife of J. Frederick Coxon. It was an "Application of Receiver for Authority to Sell Real Estate and Personal Property and Chattels." It is not known why Vivian was the primary agent in the court proceedings.

This was the beginning of the end for the Coxon Belleek China Company.

The court records state:

Andrew L. Faban, Receiver, represents to the Court that there is still in his hands personal property and respectfully recommends an order to be entered directing that so much of the same remains unsold at the time of the public sale. It includes a mortgage of $18,000.00, together with the accrued interest thereupon in favor of the Wooster Board of Trade. It also includes Palm Fechteler and Company obtained a judgment against the Coxon Belleek Company and had an execution issued and a levy made on the property of said company, and Vivian K. Coxon obtained a judgment against the Coxon Belleek Company, both of which judgments were obtained prior to the appointment of the receiver.

Personal property owned by the Coxon Belleek China Company as shown on the Inventory and Appraisement hereto filed will not be of sufficient value when sold to pay all of the liabilities of the company, which so far, as your receiver is presently advised, amount to

about $250,000.00. The receiver may be ordered to advertise and sell the personal property.

Vivian Coxon, the Plaintiff resides in Wooster, Ohio, and is a stockholder of the Defendant Corporation. She also is a creditor of said Defendant Corporation, holding unpaid promissory notes by it executed in the aggregate principal amount of $22,200.00. The Plaintiff files this application on behalf of herself and all other creditors. The Defendant, the Coxon Belleek China Company, is a corporation organized and existing under the laws of the state of Ohio, with its principal place of business in Wooster, Ohio. It was incorporated on November 5, 1926, with an authorized capital stock of 1,100 shares, divided into 500 shares of preferred stock of the par value of $100.00 per share and 600 shares of common stock without par value. Of the capital stock authorized, 250 shares of preferred stock have been issued and 500 shares of common stock. The total obligations of the corporation amount to approximately $233,394.54, of which amount $21,819.00 is represented by promissory notes secured by mortgage of the corporation's manufacturing plant in Wooster, Ohio, $220,020.88 consists of unsecured promissory notes, $4,880.00 of bills payable unsecured, taxes of $2,189.16, and payrolls unpaid of $2,685.50. The assets of the corporation consist largely of real estate, machinery, tools, shop fixtures, and equipment, all of which property is under mortgage to the Wooster Board of Trade, and of accounts and notes receivable merchandise and stock in trade. The total amount of its current assets is small and is of doubtful value.

The corporation first established its manufacturing plant in Wooster, Ohio approximately four years ago. Its present total obligations represent for the most part expenditures incident to the creation and establishment of a new business and going concern. By reason of such expenditures, its current assets have been reduced to an amount wholly insufficient to meet its current liabilities. Payrolls and taxes are past due and unpaid, and there is now no money available to pay them. Of its prior obligation, more than $200,000.00 is now past due and unpaid. It is unable to renew them or obtain extensions of time. It is operating under the constant danger of being forced to suspend entirely by *the enforcement of claims of creditors. It is moreover in urgent need of additional funds to meet current operating expenses. It will be able to dispose of its entire production at a profit to the corporation and will be able to meet its current bills, reduce its prior indebtedness, and increase its assets only if operation is continued.*

Palm Fechteler and Company of New York, one of its creditors has secured a judgment against said corporation in the amount of $570.43 and costs, and such property is now advertised for sale by the Sheriff of this County on July 1, 1930, under execution levy. Unless a receiver is appointed, other creditors will obtain judgments on their claims and levy executions against the corporation's plant and cause it and all of their property to be sold piece meal under unfavorable conditions at a fraction only of its actual value."

The June 27, 1930 court case was the first in a succession of court cases regarding the demise of the Coxon Belleek Company culminating in the sale of all the assets and closing of the company. On September 12, 1931 in the case of Vivian Coxon vs. The Coxon Belleek China Company, Andrew L. Faban, receiver for the Coxon Belleek Company was given the authority of the court to sell at public auction the personal property and real estate belonging to the Coxon Belleek China Company. "It is ordered that Andrew Faban as receiver shall offer at public sale all the personal property remaining undisposed on the date of the sale and all the real estate belonging to the Coxon Belleek China Company.

On November 4, 1931, the Coxons sold their property back to the Wooster Board of Trade, and the corporation was dissolved in September 1932.

The Coxon Belleek Company, among the makers of the finest china ever made, was relegated to history.

Two companies tried to take over the business after the Coxon failure. The first was Wooster Vitrified China Company headed by a man by the name of Flannigan. This firm made restaurant china, but it didn't last long. Next, Herbert Cruse resumed operations, making mostly vases. He also folded soon after he began.

Wayne County records show that the Wooster Board of Trade again sold the Coxon Company to the Wayne Potteries on August 31, 1935. There is no documented information about this company.

Shortly after that, an article in the *Wooster Daily Record* entitled, "Local Man Buys Wooster Pottery," says:

Horace Crew, former General Superintendent of A.E. Tile Company has purchased the personal property and equipment of Wayne Potteries, Inc. at Wooster, it was announced here today. The Wayne plant originally was created for the Coxon Belleek China Company, which was soon taken over by the Wooster Pottery Company; and subsequently was acquired by the Wayne Potteries, Inc. He will take possession around July 1. Crew recently purchased a mortgage from the Wooster Board of Trade on the real estate of the Wayne Potteries and at the present, has a foreclosure suit pending in the courts.

However, this company was not in business for long, and was the last china and pottery company to be located at the site.

Kenneth Markham of Canal Fulton, Ohio wrote an article published in the June 13, 1962 *Daily Record* about the Coxon Belleek company and its demise.

The finest stores in the country were retailers for Coxon Belleek China. The Depression came and the firm became defunct. It was too young in industry to survive and their product was too much of a luxury. Moreover, the Coxons lost their money and could not carry the firm. It was most unfortunate because connoisseurs claimed Coxon's quality was unsurpassed. The story of Coxon Belleek's endeavor is short and tragic for those interested in the firm. But those fortunate to have this ware value it now as collector's items.

The Great Depression was the most significant factor for the closing of the Coxon Belleek China Company in 1931. It produced a product that was too high priced a luxury for depression times.

According to Regina Lee Blaszczyk in her book, *Imaging Consumers: Design and Innovation from Wedgwood to Corning,* she says "Declining demand [due to the

Depression] forced many companies to shut their doors. Between 1922 and 1929, the average household spent 6.8% of its annual budget on china and glassware, expenditures that paled next to those from the previous era 1898–1916 when consumers spent thirteen percent of their incomes on tableware. Retailers ordered less and less pottery every year."

Frank Hawe in an article titled, "Product Design: The Answer to Price Advance" reflected on the difficulties in the early 1930s. "Here was a buyer's market without buyers. Prices knew no bottom in the battle for survival. The outlook for both Manufacturers and Dealers was a persistent blue until the end of the fiscal year when the deficit gave it a distinct reddish cast."

Ward Konkle reports, "At the time the manufacture of Coxon Belleek china stopped in Wooster, a number of local people expressed the belief that if the Coxons' skill in financial management had matched their skill in making fine china, the company would still be in business today. This opinion seemed valid when one considers that Walter Lenox of Trenton went through the same depression, but because of his shrewd management ability, the company still thrives today, despite the fact that he became blind a few years after he parted company with Jonathan Coxon Sr."

However, further research makes clear that neither "poor management" nor "poor financial management" were a factor in the demise. The three Coxons, brothers Fred and Edward, and Edward Jr., brought decades of management and production experience to the new enterprise. In addition, the brothers brought a significant amount of financial backing in starting the company. They bought all of the equipment, the building, the raw materials and paid for the employee start-up expenses. When the company was dissolved in late 1931, unsecured debts totaled over $220,000, a sizeable sum (in 2007 terms, that would be the equivalent of $2,647,035).

Although by 1930, Lenox had developed a highly influential ivory-body dinnerware, received a White House commission, and produced many stylish patterns, even they struggled to stay open during the Depression. Lenox executives took large pay cuts and the workforce took smaller ones. The company kept experimenting with new alliances with other industries and with new products: lamp bases, tableware decorated with low-relief modeling rather than costly colored decals or gilding, china inserts for metal dish holders, perfume bottles and atomizers, and x-ray spools and transformer shields for Westinghouse. Lenox had many advantages over Coxon Belleek. It had been in business for thirty-five years compared to less than five for Coxon Belleek. It had the ability to add new products to carry them over the tough times. And, due to its longevity and reputation, it had built a reservoir of customer satisfaction and credibility in the market. Tough competition to beat!

The Great Depression was not the only reason for the failure of Coxon Belleek. There were several other factors, when combined with the Depression, spelled the death knell of Coxon Belleek. The book *China and Glass in America 1880–1980*, shares that "the economic collapse of the Great Depression advanced designers and the role of product design within the tableware industry. Manufacturers who had improved profits in the 1920s through greater efficiency watched their gains evaporate as consumers stopped buying." Never before had fashion and style mattered so much. Women made the vast majority of household purchases, some eighty percent. In the 1920s, they shopped with heightened expectations in terms of style, novelty and quality. "As the 'new American tempo' rapidly transformed consumer society during the late twenties, factories making everything from automobiles to clothing and furnishings scurried to increase output, lower prices and hasten the pace of design and innovation. The American consumer was enmeshed in design fever."

Coxon Belleek patterns, for the most part, were static and based upon historic designs. This flew in the face of the emerging desire for new and innovative designs desired by the consumer. Starting in the mid-twenties, the wave of Modernism swept across the home furnishing trade. And Coxon Belleek lost sight of the emerging desires of the consumer even though it manufactured a high quality product respected by all in the industry.

Another modern initiative eluded the management of Coxon Belleek to their detriment. China and Glass in America 1880–1980 states,

> The emergence of professional advertising agencies after WWI brought traditional efforts together with a host of new strategies. Manufacturers traditionally advertised at the local level in the various trade publications like Pottery Glass and Brass Salesman, American Pottery and Glass Reporter and China Glass and Lamps. However, national advertising firms propelled manufacturers who could afford the cost directly into millions of American homes through newspapers, radio and above all popular magazines. Starting around WWI, advertisements associating fine living with china and glass began to appear. By the 1920s and 1930s many tableware makers used advertising to entice customers to purchase their products at local stores. From Pyrex to Steuben and from Homer Laughlin to Lenox, American readers were bombarded by declarations of how new dishes would improve their lives.

Coxon Belleek advertised very little. They barely advertised in the trade publications, and there is no evidence that they advertised in any national magazine aimed at the consumer. A rare ad in the Wooster Daily Record was their only public advertising voice. Either the cost for advertising was determined to be too high, or they felt that they didn't need to advertise. Speculation is that Coxon Belleek relied heavily on their relationships with the jewelry stores and department stores that sold their china, and felt that this gave them sufficient exposure.

Another influence on the industry in the 1920s and into the 1930s were the buyers from the larger department stores and highest quality jewelers; the precursors of the Wal-Mart equation: the demand of lower and lower prices from each manufacturer in order to pass on these lower prices to the consumer. They acted as the ultimate traffic cop: if a manufacturer wanted to exhibit their wares in a high class or high volume store, they demanded that prices must be cut. If the prices were not cut to the satisfaction of the buyer, then the manufacturer was not permitted to sell their product in that store.

According to Regina Lee Blaszczyk, "During the 1920s, several factors—rising energy costs, high union wages, railroad shipping boycotts, a flood of cheap Japanese imports, and shifting demand—eroded the prosperity that the Great War had brought to many United States potteries." These factors alone would have placed significant pressure on the potential success of Coxon Belleek. When you add the changing desires of the consumer for more colorful and jazzy designs, inability to develop alternate products, gatekeeping by the store buyers to demand lower prices, and very little advertising, Coxon Belleek had an impossible mountain to climb toward financial success. The high quality of their product just wasn't enough to continue in business.

SOURCES:

/// Ward Konkle, "The Demise of Coxon Belleek," The Daily Record, Wooster, Ohio.

/// Kenneth Markham of Canal Fulton, Ohio in his regular news column published in the June 13, 1962 The Daily Record, Wooster, Ohio.

/// China and Glass in America 1880–1980, "Imaging Consumers: Design and Innovation from Wedgwood to Corning," by Regina Lee Blaszczyk.

/// The Daily Record, Wooster, Ohio.

/// Common Pleas Court, Wayne County Ohio.

FAMILY BREAKUP AND TRAGEDY

The dissolution of the Coxon Belleek Company took a major toll on the Coxon family members involved in the company. The three family members, brothers J. Frederick, Edward T., and Edward's son Edward B., all suffered in varying degrees as a result of starting and then dissolving the company.

The two brothers, and probably to a certain extent the son Edward, brought a sizeable amount of financial support to start the company. Each had worked at the very successful business, Great Western Pottery of Kokomo, Indiana, for many years. Edward T. started with the company in 1893 and Fred followed in the late 1890s. Edward B. also worked for the company for approximately ten years. J. Fred worked for Great Western as well as forming several successful companies in the Wooster area prior to starting the Coxon Belleek Company. When Coxon Belleek was dissolved in late 1931, the unsecured debt was over $220,000 an equivalent of $2,647,035 today. Undoubtedly, the three Coxons shared the majority of this unsecured debt.

The person with the most experience in the china and pottery industry was Edward T. Coxon who served as the Treasurer of Coxon Belleek. Edward T. was trained in the pottery

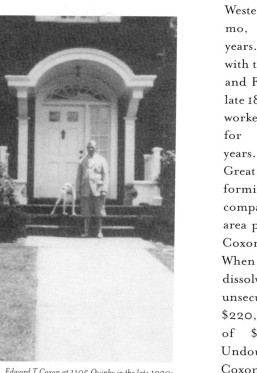
Edward T Coxon at 1105 Quinby in the late 1920s

business by his father, Jonathan Coxon the founder of the Lenox China Company of Trenton, which was known at that time as The Ceramic Art Company. Beginning at the Great Western Pottery Company in 1893, by 1925 he was fifty-five years old and had retired from management at Great Western. Having lived in Kokomo for over thirty years, one wonders why he was enticed to move to Wooster, invest a sizeable amount of money in a new china company, and enter into the position of Treasurer with the attendant pressures. Edward T. moved to Wooster with his wife Mary in 1925–6 and lived at 1637 Beall Avenue. Articles written about him as well as his wife indicate that both of them were highly respected in the Kokomo community. He was referred to as a "community leader" and she was much beloved.

John Frederick, known as Fred, was born in 1879 and in 1925 was forty-six years old. J. Fred was also trained in the pottery business by his father, Jonathan Coxon. As President of Coxon Belleek, he also brought much experience to Coxon Belleek. In addition, Fred had an entrepreneurial bent with a history of starting new and successful companies. After working for his father in Trenton, he moved to Kokomo, Indiana and worked with his two brothers at Great Western Pottery. He then moved to Tiffin, Ohio in 1900 at the age of twenty-one, appointed as Superintendent of the Tiffin branch plant of Great Western Pottery. In 1916, while still working for Great Western, he organized the Wooster Pottery Company based in Fredericksburg, Ohio, which grew with multiple branches in Salem, Ohio and Clarksburg, West Virginia. Wooster Pottery was renamed the Wooster Sanitary Pottery Company in the early 1920s. Fred moved to Wooster in 1916 and lived at 702 North Bever Street in Wooster with his wife Vivian and family. In 1924, he severed his relationship with Wooster Sanitary Pottery and began the process of starting Coxon Belleek. While he was President of Coxon Belleek, starting in 1925, he also became President of the Wooster Feed Company. He continued as President of both companies until 1928 when, according to his grandchildren George A. Limbocker Jr., and Rebecca Coxon Dyson, he suffered a serious stroke. He moved to St. Petersburg, Florida to recover and then moved to his wife's family home in Albion, Michigan in 1937. After his stroke, he was not able to return to Wooster and take an operational role with either company. When he died in 1951, he remained a member of the Board of Directors of the Wooster Feed Company. He was highly respected in Wooster as a churchgoer, a member of several lodges and temples, and was one of the founders and first President of the Kiwanis Club of Wooster, Ohio.

Not as much is known about Edward B. Coxon except that he also brought his share of practical experience in the pottery industry. Edward B. was the son of Edward T. and worked for Great Western Pottery for over ten years before he moved to Wooster. He was the Plant Manager for the Coxon Belleek Company. He lived at 1105 Quinby Avenue in Wooster with his wife Anita.

What happened to them after the demise of the company?

The son Edward B. had the largest disappointments and life setbacks. With the financial disaster, he lost his house on Quinby Avenue and his wife Anita filed for divorce on August 4, 1931. Records from the Court of Common Pleas, Wayne County, Ohio indicate that a Decree of Divorce was filed on October 23, 1931 with Anita Coxon, Plaintiff and Edward B. Coxon, Defendant. They were married on the eighteenth day of February, 1925. "Defendant has been guilty of gross neglect of duty toward Plaintiff and Plaintiff is entitled to a divorce as prayed for. Plaintiff is hereby

restored to her maiden name of Anita Cahill."

Edward B. moved in with his parents in their house on Beall Avenue and then left Wooster with his parents and moved back to Trenton, New Jersey. Then, on September 14, 1936, the Wooster Daily Record reported,

Edward B. Coxon dies suddenly. Former Wooster China Company executive succumbs in Trenton, New Jersey hospital. Telegrams received by Wooster friends this morning brought word of the death of Edward B. Coxon, former resident of Wooster, and son of Edward T. Coxon, who now lives in Trenton, New Jersey. Mr. Coxon died Saturday in Trenton after a short illness. Mr. Coxon, with his father and his uncle, J.F. Coxon, established and operated the Coxon Belleek China Company in this city, a plant that made a grade of chinaware that was unsurpassed anywhere. Because of its limited market, the backers, although they invested large sums of money in perfecting their product and organization, were never able to manufacture and market it at a profit. After they released their ownership of the plant, it was fitted to make a more popular and less expensive line of goods. Edward B. Coxon, during most of his residence in Wooster, lived for a number of years on Quinby Avenue. He was an only son. His father and mother resided at 1637 Beall Avenue, the mother passing away not long after they went to Trenton from Wooster. The Coxons came to Wooster from Kokomo, Indiana.

Edward B. died prematurely in his early forties with a broken heart and a sense of failure.

His father Edward T. also suffered significant life changes. After the company folded, it is clear that Edward and Mary suffered major financial setbacks. Their son Edward moved in with them after his divorce, and then on December 24, 1932, the Peoples Savings and Loan Company initiated foreclosure of their home with an appraised value of $27,500.00. On March 27, 1933, the appraisal was set aside and a new appraisal was ordered because the house didn't sell. Finally, in May 8, 1933, in the Court of Common Pleas, the final case of the Peoples Saving and Loan Company, Plaintiff vs. Mary B. Coxon, et al., Defendants was decided.

Said proceedings and sale are hereby approved and confirmed. The said sheriff is ordered by a deed duly

Edward B Coxon & Anita Cahill c. 1925

property in their hands or under their control that belong to said corporation. The sheriff is hereby enjoined from selling any property of the said Coxon Belleek Company and is hereby directed to surrender any and all property now in its possession under execution, levy or otherwise to said Andrew L. Faban, as such receiver. Said receiver is hereby authorized to continue the business as a going concern to operate the same and manage its assets and do all things necessary in order to preserve said property and continue the business of said corporation. Upon motion of the plaintiff, it is being made to appear to the satisfaction of the court that the Wooster Board of Trade of Wooster, Ohio, Palm Fechteler & Company and Vivian Coxon are necessary parties to a complete determination of the questions arising in the above-entitled action. It is ordered that the said Wooster Board of Trade and Palm Fechteler & Company are hereby made party defendants herein.

executed to convey said premises to the purchaser, The Peoples Saving and Loan Company. Free from any dower estate. It is further ordered that our of the proceeds of said sale, the purchaser pay first to the Treasurer of Wayne County the sum of $1,063.28, being the taxes, penalty and interest due on said premises. Secondly, to the Clerk of this Court, the costs of this action, taxed at $72.62. Thirdly, to the Plaintiff, The Peoples Savings and Loan Company, the balance of said purchase money, the sum of $13,864.10.

Then, in order to obtain all other assets of Edward T. and Mary, it is further ordered the sheriff pay the purchaser in possession of said premises that the Clerk have entered on the margin of monies, closes and action, credit, stocks, contracts and other assets of every kind, and all other property, real, personal, or mixed, to have and to hold the same pursuance and of under the orders and direction of this court. Said receiver is hereby authorized and directed to take immediate possession of all and singular the property and assets above described. All officers, directors, agents and employees of the defendant, The Coxon Belleek China Company, are hereby required and directed to forthwith turn over and deliver to such receiver, or his duly representatives, all

Court records are no longer extant to clarify Vivian's role as creditor. She may have been owed money if Fred sold his shares to Edward T. and Edward B., or she may have been a creditor in her own name, as she inherited property in Michigan from her parents.

Broke and disillusioned, Edward T. and Mary left Wooster and moved back to Trenton, New Jersey. They never returned to Kokomo where they had lived for over thirty years. Mary died in 1933, shortly after they returned to Trenton. Edward T. died in 1941 after suffering the loss of his wife and the unexpected loss of his son, Edward B. in 1936.

John Frederick, known as Fred, appeared to emerge less damaged financially, but his health was definitely impacted. In 1928, he was forced to resign as both President of Coxon Belleek and Wooster Feed Company because of a serious stroke, curtailing his active leadership role in the Coxon Belleek company and never returned to live in Wooster. J. Fred's precipitous health setback may have spelled the beginning of the end of the Coxon Belleek Company. Fred was the entrepreneur of the three, was the leader of the company (signified by his role as President), and was in the prime of his working career at the age of forty-nine. His older brother Edward was almost sixty years of age and in the twilight of his career. Fred must have felt the attendant pressure involved in his decision to entice his brother and his brother's son to Wooster to start the Coxon Belleek Company with him only to be forced to retire prematurely from the company because of his health. Ultimately, both Edwards, father and son, left Wooster broke and heartsick. For a family as close as the Coxons, this may have caused the deepest personal setback for Fred. Fred was able to continue as Director of the Wooster Feed Company until his death, but moved to Florida an unwell man who was forced to leave his active role with the company of his dreams. Fred lived until 1951.

One can only speculate about the reasons that these three men and their families came to Wooster to start the Coxon Belleek Company. However, clear threads of family cohesiveness, business acumen, hard work and diligence, entrepreneurial spirit, and family pride are strongly evident. One senses that Fred convinced his brother Edward and Edward's son to pack up their families and come to Wooster to start this new venture. But why did they leave Kokomo where they had sunk roots and commanded much community respect? Could it have been a latent Coxon family competition with Walter Lenox and his Lenox China Company? The Coxons already possessed the formula to make high quality Belleek china, and they may have felt that they could equal or surpass the Lenox China Company in quality and success. The Roaring 20s were a time for entrepreneurs and optimists. Everything could be accomplished with hard work, experience and knowledge of business. The three Coxons possessed all of these.

The Great Depression negatively affected every part of the country and the world. The Wooster branch of the Coxon family came to Wooster excited about the future, successful, wealthy, and well respected. They left Wooster with ill health, financially destitute and heartbroken, never able to recover their prior success and entrepreneurial spirit.

This is but one of many family and business stories from the Depression. It is heartbreaking and poignant, but the beauty of Coxon Belleek china is a testament to their abilities and entrepreneurial spirit. ⁄⁄

CONCLUSION

Vincent Boomheld, chair of the art and design committee of the United States Potters Association, spoke at the 1942 annual meeting and said,

Although the U.S. market for china and glass tableware is enormous compared to other places around the globe, the American producer has been relatively small compared to manufacturers of automobiles, structural steel and other industrial goods. But the products of the tableware makers are among the most appealing of home furnishings, and the changes that have unfolded industry-wide over the past century are dramatic. Tariffs, invention, and automation, designer marketing and the persistence of craftsmanship offer fascinating stories and the entrepreneurial nature of these industries is exhilarating. While few fortunes have been made by manufacturing glass or china, many have been lost. Numerous individual potteries and glass houses have prevailed over long periods of time, but the general story of the industry is one of struggle and decline during the twentieth century, using widely disparate market strategies, glass companies like Lenox, Libby and Corning, and potteries like Lenox China and Homer, Laughlin China have survived depressions, wars, and foreign and domestic competition. All of these firms have been blessed with inspired thinking and critical junctures. Ultimately, however, no history of a single company can account for the complex story of china and glass production in America.

Mr. Bloomfield was talking about an industry, but he could also be talking about one company: Coxon Belleek. Coxon Belleek manufactured among the highest quality of china in American history. This small company started with the brightest of futures and faded away with disillusionment and defeat. It is a microcosm of the transition from the heights of the Roaring 20s to the depths of the Great Depression. This story is about a company and a family. Both will be remembered for the quality of their product, and if they were to be remembered for one accomplishment, quality of work is a magnificent and enduring legacy.

SOURCES:

// Victor Boomheld, speech, 1942.

CATALOGUE

IVORY PLAIN

IVORY WITH GOLD BANDS

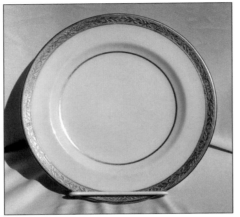

Ivory with Gold Bands and Color

Floral Plain &
Floral with Color Bands

Floral
with Gold Bands

Floral with Gold Bands and Color

Italian Vista

"WARRIN"

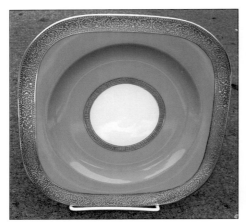

"Boulevard"

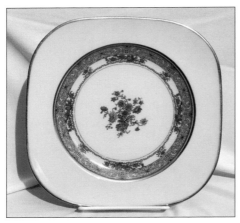

BUMBLEBEE

"Iota"
and Enameled Decorations

Mistletoe
with Flowers

CARNATION

CUSTOM DESIGNS

CUSTOM FLORAL DESIGNS

Scalloped Plate

COFFEE & TEA SETS

Egg Cups

Dinner Place
Name Tags

Salt Cellars

FULL TABLE SETS

Catalogue Notes

/// The "Iota" and the "Boulevard" patterns are the only named patterns of the Coxon Belleek Company. All other patterns were distinguished through a combination of letters and numbers. The pattern numbers corresponded to the individual decal designs bought from the Palm & Flechter Company of New York. All or part of the letters corresponded to the colors used in the individual patterns.

/// The "Warrin" designation, included with the logo on some of the patterns, came from Edmondson Warrin, Inc. of New York, a company that specialized in custom sterling silver, gold and silver deposits, monograms and crest designs. It is unknown whether Coxon Belleek contracted with Edmondson Warrin or vice-versa. The two companies were obviously partners in the development of several patterns.

/// The remainder of the patterns identified here—Italian Vista, Bumblebee, Mistletoe with Flowers and Carnation—were named by the author to make it easier for the reader to recognize common patterns.

/// The patterns identified here as "Custom" were likely developed for individual customers through a unique order of one-of-a-kind sets of china.

Price List for Pattern D-1025
(Rose or Bouquet Pattern)

Plates

A	Dinner Plate (10⅜"w)	$27–35
	Luncheon Plate (9")	$23–28
	Salad Plate (8¼")	$17–21
	Salad Plate (7¼")	$16–20
	Bread and Butter Plate (5¾")	$11–14
B	Square Dessert Plate (7⅞")	$32–38

Bowls

B	Cereal Bowl (5⅞")	$21–25
	Fruit/Dessert (Sauce) Bowl (5")	$15–18

Tea and Coffee

C	Sugar Bowl with Lid	$40–75
	Creamer	$35–68
	Tea Pot	$150–210 (rare)
	Cup and Saucer Set (Flat)	$25–32
	Cup and Saucer Set (Footed)	$30–38
D	Coffee/Chocolate Pot	$165–235 (rare)
E	Demitasse Coffee/Chocolate	$30–38
	Cup and Saucer Sets	$25–32
F	Cup (double handle) and Saucer Set	$50–75 (rare)

Soups

	Rimmed Soup Bowl (8⅜")	$25–30
G	Soup/Bouillon Handled	$40–60

Serving Pieces

H	Oval Vegetable Bowl (8½")	$36–42
	Oval Vegetable Bowl (9⅜")	$42–48
	Oval Vegetable Bowl (10")	$48–55
	Oval Candy Dish (8⅛" x 4¼")	$34–38
I	Oval Vegetable Bowl with Lid	$58–68
J	Round Handled Vegetable Bowl with Lid	$88–125 (rare)
K	Oval Serving Platter (10¾")	$40–60
	Oval Serving Platter (12⅞")	$45–68
	Oval Serving Platter (14⅞")	$60–85
L	Handled Cake Plate (9¼")	$60–85
	Handled Cake Plate (10¼")	$100–150 (rare)
M	Footed Gravy Bowl	$52–64

Special Pieces

N	Salt	$17–25
O	Table Name Plate	$52–75 (rare)
P	Napkin Holder	$20–28
	Poached Egg Cup	$123–175 (rare)
Q	Scalloped Plate	$75–125 (rare)

Percentage increase over/under

the D-1025 pattern *(for individual pieces)*

Ivory	Less 10%
Boulevard and Iota	Same
other Flowered Patterns	Plus 15%
other Formal Patterns	Plus 20%
Unique one-of-a-kind Patterns…	
	Plus 50–100% (rare)

Full Sets of 12 with Multiple Serving Pieces

Ivory

$1,800–2,200

D-1025	$2,100–2,450
Boulevard and Iota	$2,100–2,450
other flowered patterns	$2,550–2,825
other formal patterns	$2,750–2,950
unique one-of-a-kind patterns...	
	$3,000–5,000 *(rare)*

/// This price list is courtesy of Sally Barnes, Jim Norton and Joan and John Bupp, long-term residents of Wooster and Wayne County and experts in buying, selling and appraising Coxon Belleek. All three submitted their price estimates independently and then the three submissions were averaged to yield the final price estimate listed above. Prices effective 2008.

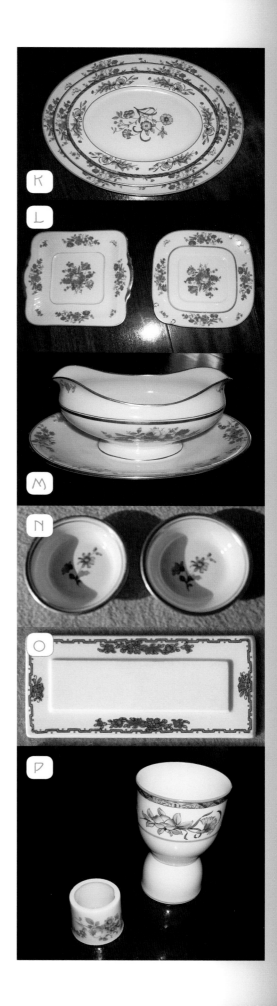

Appendices

Vignette: The Tragic Story of Nellie Coxon

1889 CERAMIC ART POTTERY OFFICIAL OPENING WITH NELLIE COXON

from *History of Lenox China*

"Despite the bleak economic situation in the ceramics industry generally, Ceramic Art Company was founded on May 16, 1889 by Walter Scott Lenox, Jonathan Coxon Sr., William S. Handcock, and Joseph Rice, with a surprising forecast. By organizing a small pottery that specialized in art porcelain, Lenox & Company sidestepped these economic and labor issues. Their product was aimed at an upper-class clientele divorced from the roller coaster crockery market, and their few employees were artists and decorated artisans without affiliation to the large National Pottery Workers Union.

"During the summer of 1889, the progress of building and outfitting their new pottery was chronicled in local newspapers and national trade journals. Finally, on Monday, August 12, a company of Trenton's prominent businessmen and pottery owners was assembled to witness the official opening of the pottery and wish the company well. Coxon's granddaughter Nellie turned on the steam and started the engine after the time-honored fashion of inaugurating a world's fair.

"Following this charming ceremony, everybody proceeded to the second floor where a tempting banquet had been spread and a social hour was spent wishing the complete success of the enterprise. Although the work force was planned to include 50 persons, only 18 were on board at the beginning to prepare the ware that would be decorated later. The modelers and molders had started to work several weeks earlier in various locations around the city, so many molds were already on hand opening day.

"By mid-October, 1889, The Ceramic Art Company was ready to exhibit its first wares, which were described as pretty, original, artistic, beautiful, elegant, and entirely fresh in design. The company's first advertisement stressed the original shapes, the superb styles of the decorated goods, and the pure white fabric especially adapted to the wants of amateur decorators. Reporters were continually impressed with the high quality of work being produced by such a small operation. Indeed, one commentator was moved to call the pottery cute because of its relation to the big potteries surrounding it."

Nellie was age two.

1910—TRAGIC TRAIN WRECK

Kokomo Tribune, Sept. 24, 1910
"Indiana Train Wreck"

"Second interurban disaster of the week in Indiana attended by several fatalities. Six persons were killed and twelve injured in a collision between a southbound freight and a northbound limited train on the Indiana Union Traction Company's line on noon today. The cars crashed together at the Restler Crossing, two miles north of Tipton, under circumstances almost identical to the tragic wreck near Bluffton on Wednesday. Dead are Dr. H. Hostzhauser, Brooklyn, New York, who was on his way to marry Nellie Coxon, and W.H. Hostzhauser, brother of the physician, who was to be best man. A clump of trees hid the approaching cars and they came together at a curve. The freight train plowed through the front of the limited, demolishing the smoker. The southbound freight car overran the stopping place. The motorman had orders to wait at the first stop north of the crossing, but overran that point, thinking he could make another switch, and ran into the northbound limited, which was in charge of Joseph Baker motorman and Ed Harrison, conductor. A sad feature of the disaster is the fact that Dr. Hostzhauser was on his way here to be married tonight to Nellie Coxon, daughter of W.H. Coxon, owner of Coxon Pottery Works, and a prominent citizen of this city. His brother was accompanying him, and was to act as the best man at the wedding."

Kokomo Tribune, Sept. 24, 1910 (Second Article) "Six Killed In Train Crash"

"In disaster near Tipton, reports agree that members of the crew disobeyed orders. Charles Dragew, train dispatcher for the Indiana Union Traction Company at this point, under whose directions the ill-fated cars were running at the time of the accident, said tonight that the extra freight had orders from him to pull into Jackson, a switch five miles north of here and about three miles north of the wreck, to wait for the limited. The supposition is that Daniel Lacy, motorman of the freight, overran his order. Lacy is not here tonight. It is said he is at Anderson, with General Manager Nickle of the IUT, or has proceeded to his home in Indianapolis."

Indianapolis Star of Indianapolis, Sept. 25, 1910

"Running at a terrific speed, the cars met about a mile and one-half north of Tipton. For a long distance north of the point where the old faded limited met the extra freight, the freight had been running down grade, and it is believed here that the motorman of the extra was going full speed in an attempt to reach a switch about 3,000 feet south of where the crash occurred. While official information is not given out by the traction people here tonight, it is believed that the freight should have stopped under its order at the last switch north of the point where the cars met. It has been stated here today by minor traction officials that the motorman of the freight car overlooked the limited in its calculations and it was said that the motorman of the freight had positive instructions to stop at the siding which he passed. It's further charged here tonight that the motorman of

the freight car should and could have known the time of the arrival of the limited at the siding, which he was apparently trying to make at the time of the accident. He, like all the other traction motorman, had a timetable showing when the limited was due. The limited, likewise, was running at high speed. Josiah Baker, the motorman on the limited, was one of the most seasoned motormen in the employ of the company. His car got out of Tipton 10 minutes late, and the passengers on the limited said the car was running at high speed from the time it cleared the limits of the city of Tipton. Because of the two-degree curve where the cars met, the heavily freighted southbound car struck the limited at a diagonal blow. The first point of contact was the left front corner of the limited and the freight plowed on through the car as deep as the partition between the smoking department and the regular day coach department. All the men killed save Baker, the motorman of the limited, were in the smoking department. All were killed instantly. B.M. Mains of Tipton, who was the conductor of the limited said it was his understanding the limited had a clear track from Tipton to Shardsville. This, it is said, being a standing order of the line. Not a passenger in the smoking compartment escaped with his life, and not a passenger in the regular compartment was killed. The impact of the cars was so terrific that the crash was heard by farmers nearly a mile away, and some of those who were killed were hurtled from the limited. A sharp, heavy piece of lumber from one corner of the limited was hurled a distance of 60 feet across a fence, and the freight of the southbound car, the baggage of the limited, and the maimed and dying were entangled in a mess of splintered timbers of the two cars. All those killed were fearfully mangled.

"Probably the saddest death was that of Dr. W.F. Holtzhausen of Brooklyn, New York. With him was his brother, Walter H. Holtzhausen, also of Brooklyn. Both were killed. The doctor was on his way to Kokomo, where on Monday he was to have been married to Miss Nellie Coxon. His brother was to have been best man at the wedding. The Holtzhausen-Coxon wedding was to have been one of the most elaborate weddings of the season at Kokomo, and it is reported here this evening that several thousand dollars were to be expended in the preparations, which were already underway. Notified of the death of her affianced husband, the grief-stricken bride and her mother hurried out of Kokomo on a traction car due at the scene of the wreck at 2:30 in the afternoon. Arriving at the scene of the death of the doctor and brother, they were informed that the bodies had been brought here and properly cared for, and heart-sick, they returned to Kokomo without coming on into Tipton, though several friends of the family who came on the same car proceeded to Tipton to see that the bodies were properly cared for here. The Holtzhausen bodies will likely remain here till tomorrow when it is expected the parents of the young men will be here. Their parents expected to be in Kokomo tomorrow or Monday for the wedding of their son. In the meantime, friends of his fiancée's family have seen that the bodies were properly cared for.

"All afternoon and this evening the Young morgue where six bodies are being held was guarded by police to keep the curious crowd from the room at which the bodies lie. Late tonight, the crowd about the morgue continued large, but the police admitted only those who showed they had business there.

"The first information of the wreck here was from farmers who lived near the track. The county hereabouts is cobwebbed with rural telephones and the news of the wreck spread rapidly. The members of the first relief party found that they had been preceded by many Tipton people who had gone to the scene in automobiles. Farmers from miles around had also hurried to the place. The latter were visibly assisting in taking the dead and injured from the cars. Some of the injured were taken to nearby farmhouses temporarily. There were no sheets with which the bodies of the dead could be covered until the arrival of the relief train."

Kokomo Tribune, Sept. 24, 1910
"Finds Lover Among Dead. Ms. Coxon, Affianced To Wreck Victim Stricken By Its Sad News."

"The W.G. Coxon home, which was to have been the scene of the wedding of Dr. William F. Holtzhausen, victim of the interurban wreck at Jackson station today, and Miss Nellie Coxon, daughter of wealthy parents, Monday evening, has been turned into a scene of mourning. Orders for decorations and special preparation for the event, purchases of orchids and carnations and boxes of cigars by the intended groom have been cancelled. Instead of the marriage feast, a funeral ceremony is being prepared. The sermon of the minister will be heard at a double funeral, that of the doctor and his brother, both victims in today's wreck.

"Directly upon hearing of the wreck, W.G. Coxon, father of the bride elect, was driven with her to the scene of the wreck. Her worst fears were confirmed. She instantly recognized the familiar figure of her lover, cold in death, and gave way to grief not comforted. Serious alarm is felt for Miss Coxon. She cannot be induced to remain quiet, but walks the floors moaning. The distress of the situation attained its climax an hour later when the parents of the dead young men, Fred B. and Mrs. Holtzhausen, arrived in Kokomo direct from New York City, accompanied by Miss. Beatrice Kraft of Brooklyn, a school friend and roommate of Miss Coxon. They came here for the wedding. The parents and their young traveling companion had been in a merry mood and talked and jested as would those who were coming for the marriage of the son to the young woman of his choice. It had been decided in advance that it would be better not to break the news to them until they arrived at the home of the Coxons, and a party of relatives of Miss Coxon, the bride-to-be. There was apparently something in the expression upon the face of the Rev. Mr. Choate which startled Mrs. Holtzhausen in the midst of greetings and the introduction of the Rev. Choate, and she demanded in grief-stricken tones, "What happened? I know something terrible has happened. Tell me about it." Mrs. Coxon, clasping Mrs. Holtzhausen in her arms, whispered the terrible news. The parents, overwhelmed with the unexpected sorrow, were grief-stricken. Later they were driven to the Coxon home. Neighbors and friends comforted and sympathized with the grief-stricken ones, and they finally withdrew in respect to a grief they could not assuage. The parents of the young men, W.G. and Mrs. Coxon, and Miss Nellie Coxon leave tonight for Brooklyn where the funeral services will be held. The bodies will be shipped from Tipton."

Kokomo Tribune, Indiana, Sept. 25, 1910
"Holtzhausen Parents Leave, Relatives of Dead Brooklyn Brothers Depart From Kokomo."

"W.G. and Mrs. Coxon, Miss Nellie Coxon, the affianced bride robbed by death, Fred and Mrs. Holtzhausen, parents of Dr. William F. Holtzhausen, whose marriage to Miss Coxon would have occurred tomorrow, and Walter Holtzhausen, two victims of the wreck, formed a funeral party leaving for Brooklyn, New York, the home of the Holtzhausen family, where it was decided to hold the double funeral instead of at the Coxon home, this city. The Coxon home was to have been decorated today for the wedding under the direction of a Chicago florist. Thousands of carnations and other beautiful flowers had been ordered of local florists for the purpose, but the order was cancelled by death. The intended bridegroom's trunk arrived at the Coxon home Friday and has not been opened. Even the cigars which he had purchased as a treat to the guests were available. The milliner's supplies for the Coxons were to have been delivered tomorrow morning, but have been withheld in the face of the terrible bereavement."

Nellie Coxon was age 23.

1981—DEATH OF NELLIE COXON

Kokomo Tribune, Jan. 15, 1981
Obituary

"Nellie Coxon. Nellie Coxon, 94, died in St. Joseph Memorial Hospital on Wednesday, January 14th. Born in Trenton, New Jersey, she was the daughter of William G. and Adele Coxon. Surviving is a sister, Adele Roseberry, of Kokomo. Two sisters and a brother preceded her in her death. She was a graduate of Castle Girls' School, Terrytown, New Jersey, a member of First Congregational Christian Church, and the Kokomo Country Club, where she was women's golf champion in the 1930s."

Nellie was 94 years old. She never married. //

VIGNETTE: MANUFACTURE OF POTTERY AND THE POTTERY TARIFF

This vignette is from a dissertation for the degree of Master of Science, Department of Geography at The University of Chicago entitled: "Pottery Production in the State of Ohio," by Anne Matilda Goebel, December, 1931, Chicago, Illinois.

Pottery production is one of the well-established industries in the State of Ohio. Two major centers in the United States engaged in the making of high-grade pottery are East Liverpool, Ohio and in New Jersey. The industry in Ohio developed from small beginnings early in the nineteenth century, and has had its greatest growth in the decade from 1917 to 1927. Since 1890, the value of Ohio pottery products has never been exceeded by those from New Jersey. Pottery products for 1925 were valued at $35,645,000.00. The pottery industry is given further prestige by the fact that in 1927, 104 of the 316 potteries of the United States were in Ohio. Statistics also show that 14,694 persons out of a total of 39,749 persons engaged in pottery manufacturing in the United States made $38,721,965.00 of the $110,597,338.00 of pottery products. This means that a third of the nation's potteries are found in Ohio, employing a third of the potters in the making of more than a third of the nation's products.

Ohio had an abundant supply of natural resources basic in pottery manufacture, that were widely distributed throughout Ohio. At an early date, there were clay working plants in many sections of the state. The native deposits gave the raw materials used in all branches of ceramic work. The early potters of Ohio were also located on navigable rivers. These river locations gave a source of water necessary for mixing clay, as well as a source of power. Ohio also benefited by the early construction of both canals and railroads. The Erie Canal was completed in 1825 and by 1860, the railroads were prevalent throughout Ohio.

The development of the pottery industry in Ohio is easily followed from the initial attempts at the making of crude pottery by the Indians, through the pioneer and into the commercial period. The presence of raw material in Ohio offered an invitation for pottery manufacture at all stages of occupancy of the State. An abundant supply of clay gave the basic material for the making of pottery. The fuel supply has been adequate from the days when kilns were heated with charcoal until the present, with facilities for transportation also keeping pace with the general trend of the times.

After 1910, there was a decided upward trend in the curve showing national production. The pottery industry had been using certain European raw materials, believing that domestic clays were chemically inadequate for the manufacture of the highest grades of ware. With the outbreak of World War I in 1914, imports of clay and foreign pottery, with the exception of those protected by high insurance, were soon curtailed. Later, the practical elimination of imports led American interests to carefully investigate home resources. Native clays and raw materials were disclosed that might well be utilized in the manufacture of a wide variety of clay products. Realizing their opportunity, American manufacturers became active in exploiting the available raw materials in improving the quality of their wares, often such activity as associated with the reduction of quality, but in this case, high standards were maintained. American manufacturers put forth every effort to reach European quality and efficiency.

Raw materials used in the making of pottery were practically all native to Ohio before the industry became so highly specialized as it is at present. Ohio ranks sixth among the states of the union in the value of mineral deposits. Clay makes up a very important item of the resources of the State. Coal, gas, petroleum, gypsum, and salt are minerals also used in the pottery industry. Quantities of raw materials of a special nature are brought in from other states and from certain foreign countries. Coal formation clay is found in connection with the coal measures of the eastern and southeastern parts of Ohio and are of the best grade for pottery manufacture. These buff-burning clays occupy an area more than 12,000 square miles. The western boundary of this producing area is marked by a line extending from the western boundary of Pennsylvania through Trumbull, Geauga, Cuyahoga, Medina, Wayne, Holmes, Knox, Licking, Perry, Fairfield, Hocking, Vinton, Pike, and Scioto Counties to the Ohio River. This field is very regular, with a slight dip from five to ten feet to the mile toward the southeast. The clay beds underlie the coal — some extend almost continuously across the entire field.

An adequate supply of fuel is one of the paramount problems in the production of high-grade pottery. From ten percent to thirty percent of the retail cost of pottery is attributable to the firing of pottery products. The fuel consumed by the pottery industry in Ohio in 1919 was 810 long tons of anthracite coal, 225,000 short tons of bituminous, 24 barrels of fuel oil, 221 barrels of gas, and 3 billion cubic feet of natural gas. All of these energy products are prevalent in Ohio.

Better grade clay came from other states and a small amount from foreign countries. Kaolin is sent from Georgia, South Carolina, and from Pennsylvania. It, along with ball clay, is imported from England. The latter is largely supplied to potteries in Ohio by the states of Kentucky and Tennessee. Flint, used in the manufacture of stoneware, is quarried in Tuscarawas and Carroll Counties. The feldspar used comes from North Carolina, Maine and Maryland, with Maryland having the best grade. The gypsum, which enters into the manufacturer of forms in which pottery is cast comes from Scioto and Erie Counties. The tin and zinc oxide used in hardening glaze are supplied by Kansas, Missouri, and Oklahoma. Tennessee, Missouri, Kentucky, and Georgia now produce barium. Cobalt blue continued to be supplied by foreign deposits in Ontario and Saxony. White lead and boracic acid used chiefly in glazes are sent in from Missouri and from the Mojave Desert in California.

Government Interest and Aid Toward Success

The general belief is that the pottery industry has been favored in the matter of tariffs. Tariff legislation has been a constant and invaluable aid to native potters in their effort to maintain a stronghold in the domestic market. Judging from the steady growth of the industry, it has fairly well offset high production costs. It has not excluded foreign pottery altogether, since even after paying the duty, it's possible to sell some grades of foreign pottery at a rate lower than it can be manufactured. In general, the tariff policy has aided in driving English goods from the American market, and has tended to bring English laborers to this country.

In 1789, the first tariff law protecting American potters levied a duty of ten percent ad valorium on imported pottery. Since then, nineteen other tariff laws have been passed containing provisions affecting pottery. The Act of 1807 really paved the way for the manufacture of pottery in the United States. When an embargo was placed on English imports during the War of 1812, potteries were developed on the Allegheny Plateau to satisfy the needs of settlers. Tariff rates increased to fifty percent in 1860, and have remained at that level most of the time. Only twice has the tariff on foreign pottery been reduced. Acts have been revised or raised to a higher level, the existing laws enabling potters to hold their industry on a fairly firm commercial basis. The reduction of 1872, threatened by a further reduction in 1882, gave cause for alarm. Finally, in 1883, duties were raised from forty percent to fifty percent and from fifty-five percent to sixty percent. The reduction of 1888 was restored in 1890 by the McKinley Tariff. The Wilson Tariff in 1894 reduced the duty from fifty-five percent and sixty percent to thirty percent and thirty-five percent. Trade being in stagnation, wages were reduced from twelve percent to twenty-five percent, and in the late 1890s, a general strike resulted. With the raising of the duty to fifty-five percent and sixty percent, pottery producers were relieved of their immediate concern as to the disposal of their wares. However, the tariff in 1913 reduced the import duty on undecorated ware from fifty-five percent to thirty-five percent, and on decorated from sixty percent to forty percent. At the time, the Working Man's Organization and National Brotherhood of Operative Potters had nearly half a million dollars in its treasury with which to fight this legislation. In the end, a seventy percent levy was placed on certain pottery products. In 1925, its members were urged not to depend entirely on tariff adjustment, but to remedy their plight through the elimination of waste, the offering of more artistic wares of a higher quality, and the instilling of a national advertising campaign. The United States Potters Association in 1929 expressed a desire that the seventy percent ad valorium duty be retained. It further desired this duty be supplemented by an additional fifteen cents per dozen on earthenware and twenty-five cents per dozen on chinaware. ⫻

Coxon Family Obituaries

Elmer Henry Kenyon   1844–1919

ELMER HENRY KENYON, Rhode Island Kenyons (Generation 8), Died Nov. 16, 1919

Born Feb. 9, 1844, Onondaga, N. Y., married December 28, 1970 to Lygustia (Emery), daughter of Amos and Sarah (Austin) Fanning. Lygustia born on August 12, 1845 at Philadelphia, N.Y. and died on Feb. 12, 1929 at Albion, Michigan.

They had three children:

Pearl Lygustia Kenyon, b. Jan. 4, 1872 and married Allen J. wilder on Oct. 30, 1895.

Elmer Othello Kenyon, b. Sept. 28, 1875 and married Nellie Trimm and then married Ermina Margaret Alvarado

Vivian Emery Kenyon, b Oct 8, 1881 and married John Fred Coxon on Oct. 2, 1906

Elmer, moved from Onondaga with his father in 1861 and was with him for three or four years in Jonesville and Albion and in the winter of 1867–68, he helped his father with hotel work in burr Oak, Illinois. He also lived in Dixon, Hillsboro and other places. Besides farming and hotel keeping, he learned the trade of stone cutting. He made and sold gravestones and monuments. The cutting was done by hand, and the dust was blown away by mouth.

In 1870, having married, he opened a marble shop in Quincy. He later added the handling of seed, coal and cement. He was in the seed business for 40 years. Several times he was elected village trustee. He was an exemplary businessman, upright, faithful and trusted by everyone.

For his daughter Pearl and her family, he built a three-story house in Albion, Michigan. In St. Petersburg, he built a cottage and set out 50 fruit trees, for his daughter Vivian. She also had the Quincy homestead.

After Elmer's death in is 76th year, his widow Lygustia lived with her daughter Pearl in Albion until her death. Her father Amos Fanning, was a well-to-do stonemason in Philadelphia, N.Y. He died a few months after the birth of Lygustia. Later, his widow married Mr. Emery. Her early childhood had been in Canada, and later she lived near Rochester, N.Y.

Lygustia Clorinda Fanning   1845–1929

Mrs. (E.H.) Lygustia Kenyon Obituary,
February 13, 1929

Mrs. E.H. Kenyon Passes Away at Daughter's Home Here

The death of one of Albion's pioneer residents occurred Tuesday evening at six o'clock when, after an illness of two weeks, Mrs. E. H. Kenyon, aged 83 years, passed away at the home of her daughter, Mrs. Allen J. Wilder, 202 South Monroe street, where she had made her home for several years.

LYGUSTIA CLORINDA FANNING was born at Philadelphia, New York, August 12, 1845, the daughter of Amos Fanning and Sarah Austin Fanning. The father dying a few months after the birth of his daughter, she lived with her grandparents until she was about four years old. At this time she came to Michigan to make her home with her mother and stepfather, Reuben Emery, at the Emery farm a few miles west of Albion, on what is now the U.S.-12 highway. From this time on she was known as Lygustia Emery, because her stepfather lavished on her every tenderness and devotion, and she regarded him with genuine filial affection.

As a child she attended the Billinghurst school near her home, and later Miss Hewett's private school, held in the old Episcopal church in Albion. Her girlhood was a happy one, and friends who knew her at that time have told of her attractive personality and charm.

December 28, 1870, she was married to Elmer Henry Kenyon who, in 1861, had come with his parents to Michigan from Onondaga, New York. Mr. Kenyon was for three years employed in Albion by Ira Reed, and it was during this period that the young couple became acquainted. Following their marriage, they established their home in Quincy, near which town Mr. Kenyon's parents were living at the time.

Within a few years the home was built in Quincy in which they lived together until the death of Mr. Kenyon in 1919. Their three children were reared in this home, and later their grandchildren regarded it as a symbol of happiness and understanding.

During this span of nearly fifty years, Mr. and Mrs. Kenyon were respected citizens of their community, interested in all that contributed to the civic and social welfare of the town. Mrs. Kenyon was a member of the Episcopal church later transferring her interest to the Union church. Not a woman who sought publicity in any way, she was, nevertheless an unusually strong, quiet force for all that was right, not only in the lives of her family but also among her many friends. Always she seemed to interpret her life in terms of what she could do for others. Under the burden of her later years of invalidism she showed remarkable sweetness and patience; and even then her interest and concern was for the welfare of those who cared for her.

Though her failing health made it necessary during the last few years for her to close her home and live with her daughters, she held to the end an undiminished affection for her old home and for her friends and neighbors. For the last year and a half, while she was living in Albion, it was one of her keenest pleasures to return occasionally to Quincy. Of the love and esteem in which she was held, of her kindness and strength of character, and of her loyal, friendly personality, her former neighbors and other friends can bear witness. It can be truthfully said that all who touched her gentle, self-sacrificing life came away the stronger for the contact; and her memory cannot die among those who knew and loved her best, because her influence will live through generations.

She is mourned by her three children: Two daughters, Mrs. Allen J. Wilder, Albion, and Mrs. J. Frederick Coxon, Wooster, Ohio, and one son, E. O. Kenyon, at present in California; and four grandchildren, Audrey K. Wilder, Albion; Elma M. Kenyon, Sturgis; Lygustia P. Coxon and Kenyon Coxon, Wooster, Ohio.

The funeral will be held Friday afternoon from the home in Quincy, with burial in the Quincy cemetery.

Mrs. (E.T.) Mary Coxon   1872–1933

Mrs. (E.T.) Mary Coxon Obituary,
April 25, 1933, Kokomo Tribune:

Mrs. E. T. Coxon dies. Former Kokomo woman expires Thursday night in Trenton, New Jersey. (Same information as last article, except as follows:)

Surviving in addition to the husband is one son, Edward B. Coxon. He, it is understood, was with his parents in Trenton. The family moved there last Christmas from Wooster, Ohio, where they had resided since leaving Kokomo five or six years ago. Mr. and Mrs. Coxon came to Kokomo a young married couple about 40 years ago, Mr. Coxon becoming Assistant Superintendent in The Great Western Pottery Company's plant, now the property of The Standard, which was established at the time. They resided here about 35 years and had a wide circle of friends and acquaintances in Kokomo. They resided for many years at West Mulberry Street where they had a handsomely appointed home. A few years ago, the family moved to Wooster, Ohio, where Mr. Coxon and his son became identified with a vitreous chinaware plant. There they remained until the end of last year where they moved to Trenton, where both Mr. and Mrs. Coxon had both been born and reared, hoping that the change would benefit Mrs. Coxon's failing health. All her Kokomo friends will be saddened by the news of her demise. She is remembered here as a woman of much personal charm, sociable, neighborly, and an interesting figure in any circle in which appeared. Recalling her in the bloom of her health, it is difficult for her friends to associate the idea of death with her and to realize she is no more.

Edward B. Coxon   1895–1936

Edward B. Coxon Obituary,
September 14, 1936, Wooster Daily Record:

EDWARD B. COXON dies suddenly. Former Wooster China Company executive succumbs in Trenton, New Jersey hospital. Telegrams received by Wooster friends this morning brought word of the death of Edward B. Coxon, former resident of Wooster, and son of Edward F. Coxon, who now lives in Trenton, New Jersey.

Mr. Coxon died Saturday in Trenton after a short illness. Mr. Coxon, with his father and his uncle, J.F. Coxon, established and operated the Coxon Belleek China Company in this city, a plant that made a grade of chinaware that was unsurpassed anywhere. Because of its limited market, the backers, although they invested large sums of money in perfecting their product and organization, were never able to manufacture and market it at a profit. After they released their ownership of the plant, it was fitted to make a more popular and less expensive line of goods. Edward B. Coxon, during most of his residence in Wooster, lived for a number of years on Quinby Avenue. He was an only son. His father and mother resided at 1637 Beall Avenue, the mother passing away not long after they went to Trenton from Wooster. The Coxons came to Wooster from Kokomo, Indiana.

Edward B. Coxon   1895-1936
Edward B. Coxon Obituary,
September 14, 1936, Kokomo Tribune:
Edw. B. Coxon Dies,
End Came Suddenly Saturday
at Trenton, New Jersey Hospital

EDWARD B. COXON, age forty, a resident of Kokomo until about ten years ago, dies at 6 o'clock Saturday evening at a hospital at Trenton, N. J. according to a message received by his Uncle, W. G. Coxon, 517 West Walnut St. While Kokomo relatives had known Mr. Coxon was in ill health, his condition had become critical only recently and the end came suddenly.

He is survived by his father, Edward T. Coxon, long an official of the Great Western Pottery Company here, now the Standard Sanitary Manufacturing Company. The mother died three years ago. The father and son had been living at 33 Delaware View Avenue, Trenton. Funeral services will be held Tuesday at Trenton and burial will be made there.

Edward B. Coxon was born in Kokomo December 28, 1895 and grew to manhood in this city. He entered the military service during the world War, serving overseas with Battery D, 325th Field Artillery. The

family moved east to engage in the manufacture of pottery after the sale of the local pottery to Standard.

William G. Coxon   1860–1937
William G. Coxon Obituary,
August 4, 1937, Kokomo Tribune:
Death Claims Master Potter Tuesday Night

WILLIAM G. COXON, noted craftsman in clay, succumbs after a long illness. He was an artist in modeling and one of the founders of the pottery industry here in Kokomo. Funeral services Friday afternoon. William G. Coxon, age 77, for many years one of Kokomo's outstanding industrial figures and civic leaders, died at his home on West Walnut Street in Kokomo. Mr. Coxon was born July 23, 1860 in Jersey City, New Jersey, the son of Jonathan and Hannah J. Coxon. He was educated in the public schools of his native city, at the same time perfecting himself in the potter's craft, which had been followed by several generations of his ancestors and of which he became an acknowledged artist, following it through all active years of a long and busy life. In September, 1885, he was united in marriage with Miss Adele L. Dotie of Brooklyn, New York, who with one son and three daughters, survives him. The son is John B. Coxon of New York, the daughters are Miss Nellie Coxon, and Mrs. T. N. Roseberry of Kokomo, Indiana, and Mrs. Mark Brown of Chicago. Surviving also are three brothers, Ed T. Coxon of Trenton, New Jersey, George Coxon of New Brunswick, New Jersey, and Fred Coxon of Albion, Michigan; and two sisters, Mrs. H. D. Trout of Trenton, New Jersey, and Mrs. Joseph Erskin of Aspinwall, Pennsylvania. At the age of 21, Mr. Coxon became Superintendent of the International Pottery Company at Trenton. At an earlier age, he spent a period with The Ceramic Art Company of Trenton, of which his father was President. He was also connected for some time with the Faience Manufacturing Company of Brooklyn, New York. After being successfully Superintendent of the Union Pottery Company of Trenton and The Clark Brothers Pottery of the same city, Mr. Coxon in 1888 was called to The Brewer Pottery Company of Tiffin,

Ohio. In 1893, he came to Kokomo, and in association with Albert V. and Fred Conradt and their father, Gottlieb Conradt, founded The Great Western Pottery Company, of which he became Superintendent. Some years later, The Great Western Pottery Company took over The Brewer Pottery Company of Tiffin, Ohio, and operated both plants until 1914, when they were merged with The Standard Sanitary Manufacturing Company of Pittsburg. Mr. Coxon continued as Superintendent of the local plant of Standard until December, 1919, when he retired. For 44 years, William Coxon was a resident of Kokomo. Throughout the period, his course was such as to acquire for him the high esteem of all acquaintances. He was enterprising, public spirited, philanthropic and kindly, yet utterly free from forwardness and ostentation. He was a generous contributor to all benevolences and an earnest, though unobtrusive helper in all civic causes. In his quiet way, this man made himself a real community asset, a citizen of worthy aspirations, helpful impulses, staunch loyalties and unsullied character. He established his worth by works, not words; his memory is one upon which will rest a gentle, but enduring radiance. Mr. Coxon's son, John B. Coxon of New York, and Mark Brown, a son-in-law, Vice-President of the Harris Trust Company of Chicago, arrived Wednesday afternoon.

Edward T. Coxon   1870–1941

Edward T. Coxon Obituary,

September 26, 1941, Kokomo Tribune:

EDWARD T. COXON passes away in Trenton, New Jersey. Once prominent in pottery circle here. Relatives here have received word of the death early Friday morning in Trenton, New Jersey of Edward T. Coxon, who resided here approximately 30 years, and was a member of the official staff of The Great Western Pottery Company before it merged into The Standard. Mr. Coxon was about 72 years of age. After leaving Kokomo about 15 years ago, he went to Wooster, Ohio, where he founded The Coxon Belleek Earthenware Company, specializing in the production of particularly fine bisque ware for table service. Later

he transferred his activities to Trenton, old home of the Coxon family. Since removing to Trenton, both his wife and only son, Edward Jr., have died. Mr. Coxon himself has been in seriously impaired health for several years. Edward T. Coxon was one of four brothers who came to Kokomo when The Great Western Pottery Plant was established here nearly 50 years ago. The other brothers were William G. Coxon, Superintendent of this plant until he retired 20 years ago; Theodore, and Fred. The last mentioned is the only one living. He resides in Albion, Michigan. Announcement of the death of Edward T. Coxon will be saddening news to all in his wide circle of acquaintances here. All recall him as a particularly fine craftsman in earthenware manufacturing, as a most genial gentleman, and an excellent citizen. It is recalled that his home here for many years was on the northwest corner of Mulberry and McCann Streets. All old neighbors will be particularly grieved to learn he is no more.

J. Fred Coxon   1879–1951

J. Fred Coxon Obituary,

September 29, 1951, Albion Recorder:

JOHN FREDERICK COXON, 72, 110 West Erie street, died suddenly at 8:30AM today at his home. Survivors include his wife, Mrs. Vivian Coxon, a daughter, Mrs. George Limbocker of Traverse City; a son, Fred Coxon of Homer; three grandchildren; and two sisters. The body is at the Marsh funeral home. Further information and funeral arrangements will appear in Saturday's Recorder.

Funeral services will occur Monday at 2:00 in St. James' Episcopal church for John Frederick Coxon, 72, retired pottery manufacturer, who died suddenly at his home, 110 West Erie street, Friday morning. He had been in failing health for some time. Rev. Fr. John F. Mangrum of Detroit will officiate, assisted by Rev. Fr. Thomas B. Aldrich, rector of St. James' church. Masonic burial services will be conducted by Murat Lodge No. 14, F. and A. M. at the Quincy cemetery. There will be a Knights Templar escort from Marshall Commandery No. 17, Mr. Coxon being a member of both organizations and also of Albion Chapter No. 32, R.A.M., Albion Council No. 54, R. and S.M., and Tadmor Temple of Akron, O.

Mr. Coxon was born June 28, 1879, in Trenton, N.J., the son of Mr. and Mrs. Jonathan Coxon. He was educated in the Trenton schools and Trenton Business college. He then learned the pottery business from his father, the founder of the Lenox China Co. of Trenton. He became superintendent of the Great Western Pottery Co. in Tiffin, O., when 21 years of age. In 1916, he organized the Wooster Pottery Co., heading it for several years, and in 1924, he formed the Coxon Belleek China Co. He retired from business in 1928 after a severe illness. Mr. Coxon married Miss Vivian Emery Kenyon in Quincy Oct. 2, 1906. They moved to Albion in 1937. While in Wooster, O., Mr. Coxon served as first president of its Kiwanis club and was president of the Wooster Feed Co. for some years. He served on the vestry of St. James' church here for several years.

Surviving are his widow, a daughter, Mrs. George Alden Limbocker, Traverse City; a son, Frederick Kenyon Coxon, Homer; three grandsons, George Alden Limbocker Jr., Frederick Coxon Limbocker and Frederick Kenyon Coxon Jr.; two sisters, Mrs. Hugh D. Trout, Trenton, N.J., and Mrs. Joseph B. Erskine, Pittsburgh; a niece Miss Audrey Kenyon Wilder, Albion; and several other nieces and nephews. Mr. Coxon's body will be at his home until services Monday.

John Frederick Coxon   1879–1951

John Frederick Coxon Obituary,
October 9, 1951, Wooster Daily Record:

Funeral services were held Monday, October 1, 1951 for JOHN FREDERICK COXON, 72, retired pottery manufacturer, who died suddenly at his home in Albion. Mr. Coxon was born on June 28, 1879 in Trenton, New Jersey, the son of Mr. and Mrs. Jonathan Coxon. He attended public schools in Trenton and also Trenton Business College. Mr. Coxon was trained in the pottery business by his father, the founder of the Lenox China Company of Trenton, which was known at

that time as The Ceramic Art Company. At the age of 21, he was made Superintendent of The Great Western Pottery Company of Tiffin, Ohio. In 1916, he organized The Wooster Pottery Company of Wooster, Ohio, of which he was the President for a number of years. This company also had branches in Salem, Ohio and Clarksburg, West Virginia. While living in Wooster, he became interested in The Wooster Feed Company and was for a number of years its President and at the time of his death, was a member of its Board of Directors. In 1924, he severed his connection with The Wooster Pottery Company, and formed the Coxon Belleek China Company. He retired from his businesses in 1928, following a severe illness. He was married to Mrs. Vivian Embry Kenyon on October 2, 1906 in Quincy, Michigan. Mr. Coxon was a member of St. James Episcopal Church, life member of Murrat Lodge and several temples. He was one of the founders and first President of the Kiwanis Club of Wooster, Ohio.

Jonathan B. Coxon   1891–1953

Jonathan B. Coxon Obituary,
March 4, 1953, Kokomo Tribune

JONATHAN B. COXON, 61, a resident of this city throughout his childhood and early manhood, died Tuesday morning in Trenton, New Jersey, where he lived in recent years. He had been ill for several months. The son of the late Mr. and Mrs. W.G. Coxon, he was born March 26, 1891 in Tiffin, Ohio. The family moved to Kokomo in 1899 when Mr. Coxon and the late Albert Conradt established The Great Western Pottery here. He was a student at Culvert Military Academy and Ohio State University. He entered the business in which his father was engaged, and for a number of years, has been connected with The American Radiator and Standard Manufacturing Company at Trenton. Surviving are four daughters.

Mrs. (J. Fred) Vivian Coxon 1881–1962

Mrs. (J. Fred) Vivian Coxon Obituary,
July 27, 1962 Albion Recorder:

Services will be held at St. James' Episcopal church here Tuesday at 2:00 for Mrs. VIVIAN KENYON COXON, a former Albionite and widow of J. Frederick Coxon. Burial will be in the Quincy cemetery.

Mrs. Coxon died Thursday, July 19, at St. Petersburg, Fla., after an extended period of failing health here. Services there were delayed until Wednesday, pending the arrival from Mexico City of a niece Dr. Audrey K. Wilder of Albion, with whom Mrs. Coxon resided at one time.

The body will arrive in Albion Sunday morning. The Marsh funeral home is in charge of arrangements. Mrs. Coxon was a native of Quincy, her parents being descendants of pioneer Branch and Calhoun county residents. She attended Quincy high school and Chicago Musical college, where she studied opera as a coloratura soprano. She married Mr. Coxon at Quincy Oct. 2, 1906.

Subsequently, the Coxons lived at Tiffin and Wooster, Ohio, where Mr. Coxon was affiliated with pottery manufacturing concerns. He organized the Wooster Pottery Co. in 1916 and the Coxon Belleek China Co. in 1924, but had to retire in 1928 after a severe illness.

The Coxons resided in St. Petersburg, Fla., until 1937 and then came to Albion, residing at 110 West Erie street and being prominent figures in the Episcopal church and club circles here thereafter. Mr. Coxon died here Sept. 28, 1951. Since 1952, Mrs. Coxon had resided in St. Petersburg.

While here, the Coxons were especially interested and aided in beautification of the St. James' church grounds. Mrs. Coxon was also a former member of the Hannah Tracy Grant D.A.R. chapter and the E.L.T. club here. She was also a former member of the Pasadena (Fla.) Women's club and St. Peter's church in St. Petersburg and active in Red Cross volunteer work as long as her health permitted.

Surviving are a daughter, Mrs. George Alden Limbocker, St. Petersburg; a son, Frederick K. Coxon, Albion; a brother, Elmer O. Kenyon, Covina, Calif.; seven grandchildren and Dr. Wilder.

Members of the Limbocker family will arrive here Monday.

Additional material regarding Vivian Emery Kenyon from genealogy study of the Rhode Island Kenyons:

Born in 1881 in Quincy, Mich., Married October 2, 1906 to John Fred, son of Jonathan and Hannah (Joshua) Coxon. Children are Lygustia Pearl Coxon, born Sept. 19, 1911; Vivian Clorene Coxon, born April 30, 1919 and died May 1, 1919; and Frederick Kenyon Coxon, born December 8, 1923.

She studied at the Chicago Musical College and Busg Temple Conservatory. She lived in Wooster, Ohio where her husband was a manufacturer of chinaware until the failure of his health. They then moved to St. Petersburg, Florida and lived at 7003 Park St. John's father is descended from a long line of potter experts in England who founded the Lenox China company in Trenton, N.J.

Frederick Kenyon Coxon 1947–1996

Frederick Kenyon Coxon Obituary,
March 15, 1972, Albion Recorder:

Funeral services will be held Thursday at two p.m. at the Briffon Funeral Home in Sanford, Fla., for FREDERICK KENYON COXON, 47, who died early Tuesday of a heart attack.

Surviving are his widow, the former Zaida Everett, and five children, Fred, Victoria, Rebecca, John and Steven, all of Sanford, and one grandchild.

Mr. and Mrs. Coxon were married in Albion on Aug. 6, 1946, and moved to Florida about eight years ago.

Mrs. Dale Everett, 209 West Erie Street, and her daughter, Mrs. Lavaye Ariss, are flying to Sanford today to attend the funeral services.

Frederick "Coxon" Limbocker   1947–1996

Frederick "Coxon" Limbocker Obituary,
May 4, 1996, St. Petersburg Times *(FL):*

FREDERICK "COXON" LIMBOCKER, 49, of St. Petersburg, died Wednesday (May 1, 1996). He came here in 1952 from his native Lansing, Mich. He was an artist. He was a graduate of Northeast High School and attended Florida State University. He was an Episcopalian. Survivors include his mother, Lygustia Limbocker, St. Petersburg; and a brother, George A. Jr., Valdosta, Ga.; a nephew and a niece.

Lygustia C. Limbocker   1911–1999

Lygustia C. Limbocker Obituary,
October 24, 1999, St. Petersburg Times *(FL):*

LYGUSTIA C. LIMBOCKER, 88, of Valdosta, Ga., formerly of St. Petersburg, died Wednesday (Oct. 20, 1999) in Valdosta. Born in Tiffin, Ohio, she came here in 1952 from Lansing, Mich., and moved to Valdosta in 1996. She attended Gulf Park College, Gulfport Miss., ands Sophie Newcomb College, New Orleans. She was a member of Cathedral Church of St. Peter, St. Petersburg, and was active with Delta Gamma Sorority. Survivors include a son, George A. Jr., Suwanee, Ga., and two grandchildren, Brian S. Limbocker, Jackson Miss., and Leslie A. Limbocker, Philadelphia.

Zaida Mae Coxon   1926–2006

Zaida Mae Coxon Obituary,
October 8, 2006, The Orlando Sentinel *(FL):*

COXON, ZAIDA MAE, 80, Clermont, passed away October 6, 2006 at her residence under the care of her family and hospice. She was born May 16, 1926 in Flint, Michigan, daughter of the late Dale and Ethel Vivian (nee Schwartz) Everett. A local resident since 1965 from Albion, MI, she was a homemaker and of Baptist faith. Her husband Frederick Kenyon Coxon preceded her in death in 1972.

Surviving are her children Frederick Kenyon Coxon Jr. and wife Mae of Tavares; Victoria Vivian Keogh and husband Keith, Windermere; Rebecca Ann Dison, Clermont; Stephen Everett Coxon and wife Kathy, Sanford and John Dale Coxon, Pierson, FL; siblings LaVerne Everett and wife Kathy, Lansing, MI; Mary Ann Peterson, Ocala and LaVaye Ariss, Washington State; 16 grandchildren and seven great-grandchildren.

Visitation and wake for Mrs. Coxon will be held from 3–7PM on Monday,

October 9, 2006 at the Dison/Coxon residence, 12440 Sunshine Drive, Clermont, FL. Flowers will be accepted, however, should friends desire, the family suggests memorial contributions to Hospice of Lake & Sumter. ⫻

Jonathan Coxon b. 1837 England
d. 1919 Trenton, New Jersey
+ **Hannah Joshua** b. 1839 Wales
  m. 1859
  d. 1918 Trenton, New Jersey
    ① **William G. Coxon** b. 1860 Jersey City, New Jersey
      d. 1937 Kokomo, Howard, Indiana
      bu. Crown Point Cemetery, Howard, IN
      + **Adele Louise Dolle** b. 1861 Brooklyn, NY
        m. 1885 Brooklyn, NY
        d. 1938 Miami, Dade, Florida
        bu. Crownpoint Cemetery, Howard, IN
        ① **Nellie L. Coxon** b. 1886 Trenton, New Jersey
          d. 1981 Kokomo, Howard, Indiana
        ② **Hannah J. Coxon** b. 1887 Trenton, New Jersey
          d. 1970 Ft. Lauderdale, FL
          bu. Crown Point Mauseleum, Kokomo, Howard, Indiana
          + **Mark Anthony Brown** b. 1889 Fairmount, Grant, Indiana
            m. 1914 Kokomo, Howard, Indiana
            d. 1968 Ft. Lauderdale, FL
            bu. Crown Point Cemetery, Howard, IN
            ① **Betty Louise Brown** b. 1917 Kokomo, Indiana
            ② **Nancy Jane Brown** b. 1919 Kokomo, Indiana
              d. 1988 Maitland, Orange, FL
              bu. Evergreen Cemetery, Barrington, IL
        ③ **Jonathan B. Coxon** b. 1891 Tiffin, Seneca, Ohio
          d. 1953 Trenton, Mercer, New Jersey
          bu. Kokomo, Howard, Indiana
          + **Rexie (---)** m. abt 1913
            ① **Eleanor Adele Coxon** b. 1915 Kokomo, Howard, Indiana
              d. 1973 Barrington, Lake, Illinois
              bu. Evergreen Cemetery, Barrington, IL
          + **Doris Sylvia** b. 1905 MA
            m. 1929 MA
            d. 1950 Trenton, Mercer, New Jersey
            bu. St. Patrick's Cemetery, Lowell, MA
            ① **Adele Marie Coxon** b. aft 1930
            ② **Sylvia Ann Coxon** b. aft 1930
            ③ **Carol Joan Coxon** b. aft 1930
        ④ **Adele Louise Coxon** b. 1896 Trenton, Mercer, New Jersey
          d. 1983 Kokomo, Howard, Indiana
          bu. Sunset Memory Gardens, Harrison, Howard, IN
          + **Thomas Noble Roseberry** b. 1900 Cleveland, Ohio
            m. 1928 Kokomo, IN
            d. 1987 Indiana
            bu. Sunset Memory Gardens, Howard, IN
            ① **Thomas N. Roseberry** b. 1929 Kokomo, Howard, Indiana
            ② **J. William Roseberry**
        ⑤ **Charlotte W. Coxon** b. 1889 Kokomo, Howard, Indiana
          d. 1904 Kokomo, Howard, Indiana
          bu. Crown Point Cemetery, Kokomo, Howard, IN
    ② **Sarah Ann Coxon** b. 1862 New Jersey
      d. 1862 Trenton, New Jersey
    ③ **Theodore Burnett Coxon** b. 1862 New Jersey
      d. 1902 Tiffin, Seneca, Ohio
      bu. Greenlawn Cemetery, Tiffin, Seneca, OH
      + **Luella Smith** b. 1862 Ohio
        m. 1894
    ④ **Frank Henry Coxon** b. 1864 New Jersey
      d. 1912 Trenton, New Jersey
      + **Never Married**

1   **2**   **3**   **4**

COXON
FAMILY
TREE

COXON FAMILY TREE

⑤ **John Matthew Coxon** b. 1866 New Jersey
d. 1878 New Jersey
⑥ **Harriet Alice Coxon** b. 1868 New Jersey
+ **Joseph Bell Erskine** b. 1872 Pennsylvania
m. 1896 Trenton, New Jersey
　① **Harold Coxon Erskine** b. 1897 Trenton, New Jersey
　d. 1972 State College, PA
　bu. Greenwood Cemetery, Sharpsburg, Allegheny, PA
　+ **Margaret J. Noble** b. 1896
　m. 1921
　d. 1972 PA
　bu. Greenwood Cemetery, Sharpsburg, Allegheney, PA
　　① **Jean Erskine**
　　② **Marjorie Erskine**
　② **Florence Erskine** b. 1900 New Jersey
⑦ **Edward Thomas Coxon** b. 1870 New Jersey
d. 1941 Trenton, New Jersey
bu. Riverview Cemetery, Trenton, Mercer, NJ
+ **Mary Burbank** b. 1872 New Jersey
m. 1894
d. 1933 Trenton, New Jersey
　① **Edward B. Coxon** b. 1895 Kokomo, Indiana
　d. 1936 Trenton, New Jersey
　+ **Anita B. Cahill** b. 1899 Indiana
　m. 1925
　Div. 1931 Wooster, Wayne, Ohio
⑧ **Anne Katherine Coxon** b. 1872 New Jersey
+ **Hugh D. Trout** b. 1871 New Jersey
m. 1905 Trenton, New Jersey
　① **Henry Trout** b. 1908 Trenton, New Jersey
　d. 1971 Trenton, Mercer, New Jersey
　② **Robert B. Trout** b. 1912 Trenton, New Jersey
　③ **Richard Trout** b. 1915 Trenton, New Jersey
　④ **Edward Stokes Trout** b. abt 1906
　d. abt 1906
⑨ **George Howard Coxon** b. 1874 New Jersey
+ **Rebecca Heddon** b. 1878 New Jersey
　① **Ruth Coxon** b. 1902 New Jersey
　+ **William H. Bollman** m. 1922 New Brunswick, NJ
　② **Audrey Coxon** b. 1903 New Jersey
⑩ **Matthew Frederick Coxon** b. 1876 New Jersey
d. 1878 New Jersey
⑪ **John Frederick Coxon** b. 1879 New Jersey
d. 1951 Albion, Branch, Michigan
bu. Quincy, Branch, Michigan
+ **Vivian Emery Kenyon** b. 1881 Quincy, Branch, Michigan
m. 1906 Quincy, Branch, Michigan
d. 1962 St. Petersburg, Pinellas, Florida
bu. Quincy, Branch, Michigan
　① **Lygustia Pearl Coxon** b. 1911 Tiffin, Ohio
　d. 1999 Valdosta, GA
　+ **George Alden Limbocker** b. 1903 Detroit, Wayne, MI
　d. 1991 St. Petersburg, Florida
　bu. Sunnyside Cemetery, St. Petersburg, Pinellas County, Florida
　　① **Frederick Coxon Limbocker** b. 1946 Michigan
　　d. 1996 St. Petersburg, Florida
　　bu. Sunnyside Cemetery, St. Petersburg, Pinellas County, Florida
　　② **George A. Limbocker**
　② **Vivian Clorene Coxon** b. 1919 Wooster, Wayne, Ohio
　d. 1919 Wooster, Wayne, Ohio

1　　2　　3　　4

③ **Frederick Kenyon Coxon** b. 1923 Wooster, Wayne, Ohio
  d. 1972 Sanford, Seminole, Florida
 + **Zaida M. Everett** b. 1926 Flint, Michigan
   m. 1946 Albion, Branch, Michigan
   d. 2006 Sanford, Seminole, Florida
    ① **Frederick Kenyon Coxon**
    ② **Victoria Coxon**
    ③ **John Coxon**
    ④ **Steven Coxon**
    ⑤ **Rebecca Coxon**
⑫ **Albert Jonathan Coxon** b. 1880 New Jersey
  d. 1889 Trenton, New Jersey

1   **2**   **3**   **4**

ADDITIONAL ARTICLES OF INTEREST

This article shared information about (Mrs. J. Fred) Vivian Coxon's ancestors in Albion Michigan. They were among the original settlers:

"Waters of Kalamazoo River Cover About all that Remains of Waterburg Village, Once Larger Community Than Albion"

The ceaseless waters of the Kalamazoo river cover about all that remains of the once prosperous village of Waterburg—a community which flourished before Albion was known.

Located three miles west of the present Albion, it was pioneered by Daniel Rositer, who homesteaded land there in 1832. Three "land patents" which he received from the government are now in the possession of Elmer Emery of 913 South Superior.

It was May 4, 1883 that Tenney Peabody and his wife and their four sons and three daughters made the first settlement on land within the present settlement of Albion. The community was called "The Forkes" and not until a village plat was laid out in 1838 was Albion granted a post office.

For a period of some years Waterburg outgrew and outranked The Forkes or Albion, during which period Daniel Rositer, as the Waterburg postmaster, carried mail daily on horseback to the settlers of the little sister community to the east.

In all Rositer, who came here from Monroe county, N.Y., acquired 600 acres of land in the three "patents" he received from the government. The first, signed by President Andrew Jackson, Nov. 5, 1833, came through the White Pigeon Prairie, Mich., government land office. The other two, dated Oct. 10, 1838, and signed by President Martin Van Buren, were issued by the land office at Bronson, Mich.

The east limits of the now vanished community began just west of the present Starr Commonwealth road and extended to a point just east of the Clough's View road, which runs north off US 12. An old Indian trail, which early settlers widened into a roadway for ox-drawn vehicles and horses, bisected the little village laid out north and south of the road and among the north shore of the Kalamazoo river.

There seems to have been about a dozen homes, mostly of log construction, in early Waterburg. But the small post office building, which was about 30 rods east of the present Harry Turner farm on the north side of US 12, was built of brick. And 30 rods east of the post office was the large Waterburg Tavern, known far and wide for its hospitality and accommodations to travelers, there was a trading post, too, but the pride of the community was a large mill, built on the south side of the river. Foundation timbers of the structure may still be seen in the riverbed and the old flume hole and tail race are evident. Apparently a bridge crossed from the north shore of the river to the mill.

The log house built by Rositer and long since gone was 30 feet west of the 108-year-old farm residence built by Reuben Emery and still owned by his grandson, Elmer Emery.

Other early settlers in the community were Daniel Hurd, Riley Youngs and John Austin, all of whom owned log houses.

Probably no one today can account for the fact that Waterburg began to decline and Albion began to grow. Possibly it was because the mill burned down and since mills in Albion and Marengo were going concerns less than three miles either way, no one in Waterburg wanted to compete with them. Or it may have been that in the early death of Daniel Rositer, the village lacked the leadership which sparked it.

Reuben Emery had come to Michigan from New York in 1838 as a young man and he went to work for Rositer. Several years after the latter's death he married Mrs. Rositer. A few years later she died, and since the Rosters had been childless, the property was inherited by Mr. Emery. Subsequently he married Mrs. Sarah Fanning, who came to the community from Canada with her two little daughters, Augusta and Rebecca, and a son, Theodore.

When a young man, Theodore went to New Mexico and as a miner and prospector he became wealthy, and occasionally visited in Albion before his death.

Augusta married Elmer Kenyon, who came to Albion from Augusta, Mich., and they had two daughters, Vivian, now the widow of Fred J. Coxon, of 110 West Erie, and the late Mrs. Pearl (Allan J.) Wilder, whose daughter is Miss Audrey Wilder, Albion college dean of women. Rebecca Fanning married Nelson Farley of Albion, an early relative of the Farley Bros., prominent South Albion orchardists.

After Reuben Emery's death his son, Elmer J. Emery, continued to operate the farm. He was one of the 21 original stockholders of the Albion Malleable Iron Co. in 1888, and the only farmer in the group. His son, Elmer, now 75, still owns the farm but has resided here about 20 years.

In his possession, in addition to the early land patents as relics of Waterburg, is an old cathedral pattern pickle bottle, 14 inches in height and 4½ inches square at the bottom. It was molded in the 1820s and is now valued at about $25 as a collector's item. He also has a small, well-preserved "Walker's Pronouncing Dictionary" which bears the signature of Daniel Rositer on the inside cover and his address as Monroe county, N.Y. Recently he took out of the old homestead a wooden cabinet bathtub manufactured in 1867 by the Marshall Folding Bathtub co. It is zinc lined and in excellent condition. A prized possession is a large oil painting of Daniel Rositer, which shows him as a young man.

The present Mr. Emery during his tenure on the farm filled in many of the old open wells and foundation openings of the early buildings which once comprised the village of Waterburg.

Both Daniel Rositer and his wife are buried in Marengo cemetery.

This article was printed to rectify a mistake by the local military selection board regarding the draft status of Edward B. Coxon:

Kokomo Daily Tribune, Tuesday, August 21, 1917

The local military selection board was today under the embarrassment of having to certify as accepted for service a man whom it had previously passed as not qualified and had issued a certificate of discharge.

This man is Edward B. Coxon, son of Mr. and Mrs. Edward T. Coxon, 920 West Mulberry Street. The board frankly admits that the responsibility for the embarrassing incident rests solely upon it and not upon Mr. Coxon. The experience was an unpleasant one for both Mr. Coxon and the board. Mr. Coxon had not sought exemption or tried in any way to influence the board into excusing him when he was given his first examination. He stood ready if accepted to respond for service. After receiving a certificate of discharge, it was rather annoying, of course, to be called back and placed on the record. The board wants it understood that the error was its own and accepts full responsibility for it. It regrets the error, for it feels it may have exposed Mr. Coxon to disagreeable comment, and is especially desirous that he be set right before the public.

This article highlights the appointment of John Coxon, son of founder W. G. Coxon as Superintendent of Kokomo Sanitary Pottery Company:

Kokomo Daily Tribune, Monday, February 2, 1925.
J.B. Coxon Is Chosen To Become Superintendent of Kokomo—Sanitary Pottery Company.

The Kokomo Sanitary Pottery Company announces that John B. Coxon, formerly Superintendent of the Kokomo plant of The Standard Sanitary Manufacturing Company, has taken the Superintendency of its plant, already being in charge. Mr. Coxon returned last week from Wheeling, West Virginia, where he has been doing special work for a pottery for several months. He is glad to back in Kokomo. The mailed announcement is taking service with the concern, it says, with Mr. Coxon's many years of experience, we feel we can now offer our trade the best two fired vitreous china sanitary ware that can be produced. John B. Coxon is the son of William C. Coxon, who for nearly 30 years was Superintendent of The Great Western Pottery here, now a plant of The Standard Sanitary Company. The young man was brought in the business and knows his way from raw clay to finished product.

This article highlights the life and retirement of William Coxon:

From the book *State of Indiana Leaders:*
William C. Coxon, Kokomo

Both the distinction deserved by a master crafts-man and the financial reward that justly follows de-voted and judicious application to an art, are enjoyed by William C. Coxon, veteran Potter of Kokomo, now retired. If ever a man had what is termed as "back-ground" for a calling, this man had it for the potters' vocation. His ancestors were followers of that craft in the British Isles for generations before ever a piece of clay was fashioned and fired in this country. His fam-ily was one of the pioneers of the industry in America, having been connected with the very earliest potteries established on this side of the Atlantic.

William Coxon, while still a youth, completed his apprentice ship in pressing ware. After serving at the bench of several concerns, he became, at the age of twenty-one, superintendent of the Interna-tional Pottery Company, Trenton, N.J. In his earlier years in the craft he spent a period with the Ceramic Art Company, Trenton, N.J. of which his father was President. This firm is now known as Lenox, Inc., Trenton, N.J., manufacturers of Lenox and Belleek China. He was also connected with the Faience Man-ufacturing Company of Brooklyn, N.Y.

After being successfully superintendent of the Union Pottery Company of Trenton and the Clark Brothers Pottery of Trenton, he went in 1888 to the superintendency of the Brewer Pottery Company, Tiffin, Ohio. In 1893 he came to Kokomo and assist-ed in founding the Great Western Pottery Company of which he was the superintendent for approximately a quarter of a century. While Mr. Coxon was super-intendent, this company took over the Brewer Pottery Company in Tiffin, Ohio and operated both plants until 1914 when the Great Western Pottery Company was merged with the Standard Sanitary Manufactur-ing Company of Pittsburgh. Mr. Coxon retired as su-perintendent in December, 1919.

In these later years Mr. Coxon spent his summers in Kokomo and his winters in Miami, Florida. He still keeps his hand in at his craft however though far removed from any need to follow it. He maintains a workshop at his home and does much modeling. He says he has an irresistible urge from time to time to get his fingers back into clay. He has to his credit many valuable designs in sanitary ware, in art objects and in novelties.

Mr. Coxon was born July 23, 1860 at Jersey city, N.J., son of Jonathan and Hannah Joshua Coxon. He was educated in public schools in his native city. In September of 1885, he was united in marriage with Adele L. Dolle of Brooklyn N.Y. To them five chil-dren were born, of whom four are living. These are Jonathan B. Coxon of Lowell, Massachusetts, Miss Nellie Coxon and Mrs. Adele Roseberry, Kokomo and Mrs. Hannah Brown, Chicago. One daughter, Charlotte, died in childhood.

Two of Mr. Coxon's brothers, J. Frederick and Edward T. operate the Coxon Belleek China Com-pany, Wooster, Ohio. Edward B. Coxon is associated with them.

Mr. Coxon is a member of the Congregational Church. His fraternal connections are with the Ma-sonic Order, in which he has attained to the 32nd degree and the Elks. He belongs to the Murat Temple, Ancient Arabic Order of Nobles of the Mystic Shrine, the Kokomo Country Club and the Miami Anglers Club.

A liberal supporter of his church and all its ac-tivities, Mr. Coxon is a generous but unostentatious contributor to all local benevolences and an ardent helper in all civic movements—a citizen of unsullied character and one who has chosen to establish his worth by works rather than by words.

SOURCES FOR ALL:

/// *Kokomo Tribune*

/// *The Daily Record,* Wooster, Ohio

/// Wayne County Ohio, Common Pleas Court

/// Rhode Island Kenyons

/// State of Indiana Leaders

VIGNETTE: WALTER LENOX

"In 1889, The Ceramic Art Company was creating dinnerware pieces that reflected the Romanesque, Baroque, Renaissance, and Gothic styles, and eventually moved on to Art Nouveau. It was founded by Walter Scott Lenox and Jonathan Coxon Sr. Mr. Lenox, who was very artistically inclined, had studied master potters since his youth, and worked as an apprentice at Ott & Brewer.

"In 1894, an ambitious Walter Scott Lenox acquired all ownership of The Ceramic Art Company from his partner, Jonathan Coxon. Then, tremendously in debt and desperately needing recognition for his company in order to stay afloat, Mr. Lenox was diagnosed with local motor ataxia, a disease that eventually caused him his sight and the use of his arms and legs. Undeterred, Mr. Lenox utilized an assistant to act as his eyes and hands while perfecting the rich, creamy slip that would become the company's trademark.

"Walter Scott Lenox founded Lenox Company, Inc. in 1906. Despite his acute disability, he had become the sole proprietor of a ceramics company, and achieved his goal of creating beautiful ivory-tinted porcelain. Furthermore, he had propelled the United States into the forefront of the ceramics industry by proving that American china could be as strong and beautiful as its foreign counterparts.

"Nevertheless, he was still not satisfied. Mr. Lenox's crowning jewel arrived in 1918 when President Woodrow Wilson asked Lenox to produce the White House's china service. Most of the previous White House residents had chosen French made Limoges patterns, and this was the first time such a prestigious opportunity had been awarded to an American ceramics company. His company worked diligently to create a gold encrusted design that not only encapsulated the strength and elegance of the United States of America, but also reflected the pride for which its creator had become known.

"Walter Scott Lenox worked consistently throughout his life. He was never absent a day from his factory, even when his disability required that he be carried in by his assistants. His vision and efforts created the foundation for a company that has since grown to embrace the entire tableware world, not only in china, but crystal, silver, collectibles and giftware.

"Walter Scott Lenox realized his dream early on, despite personal tragedy and professional setbacks. His perseverance proved that American ceramics could be as resilient and durable as their British counterparts. Upon his death in 1920, Mr. Lenox had created a china legacy that even today is renowned the world over for its fine craftsmanship and superior quality."

SOURCE

// History of Lenox China,
Replacements Unlimited.

Beall House at the Wayne County Historical Society

ABOUT THE AUTHOR

DAVID BROEHL grew up in New Hampshire and came to Wooster, Ohio in 1965 to attend The College of Wooster. He fell in love with Wayne County and the city of Wooster. He has been a resident ever since.

Over the years, David became interested in glass, china and pottery and became a member of the Wayne County Historical Society. Having served in several leadership positions for the Society, he co-chaired the Coxon Belleek exhibit at the Society in the 1990s.

For David, this exhibit ignited a heightened interest in the Coxon Belleek Company. He currently chairs the permanent exhibit of Coxon Belleek at the Society and is constantly endeavoring to add new Coxon Belleek patterns to the Society's collection.

David is married to Margo and has three adult children, Nate, Julie and Dan.

The Wooster Book Company is committed to protecting the environment and to the responsible use of natural resources. The Wooster Book Company is a member of the Green Press Initiative, a nonprofit organization dedicated to supporting publishers in their efforts to reduce their use of fiber obtained from endangered forests. *Coxon Belleek: Wooster's Elegant China* is printed on 50% post-consumer recycled paper that is manufactured through a chlorine-free process.

The Wooster Book Company works with printers such as Wooster Printing & Litho that are also members of the Green Press Initiative and who help establish the chain-of-custody for this initiative by supporting best practices developed by the Forest Stewardship Council.